DAY OUTINGS

DAY OUTINGS

IDEAS AND SUGGESTIONS FOR EVERYONE

A Colourmaster/Planned Action Publication
Printed by Photo Precision Ltd, St Ives, Huntingdon, England

FIRST PUBLISHED 1973

©
JOINTLY PUBLISHED IN GREAT BRITAIN BY
COLOURMASTER INTERNATIONAL (PHOTO PRECISION LTD), ST IVES, HUNTINGDON, AND
PLANNED ACTION, 12 DENE WAY, SPELDHURST, TUNBRIDGE WELLS, KENT
COMPILED BY HARRY STONE AND E. ALAN SMITH
ISBN 0 85936 004 0

FOREWORD

Every weekend thousands of British families take to their cars, seeking a break from the humdrum of work and household chores. Trains and coaches are also transporting the bored, the curious, the fun loving, the athletic, the lazy and the adventurous. They are all intent on that great British pastime, the 'day out'. It is as traditional as 'roast beef' or 'fish and chips'.

How many parents have wracked their brains to find something or somewhere to amuse, occupy or inform their offspring? To them and countless others who are in search of the pleasure of a day out this book is dedicated.

Each chapter contains a selection of the various attractions to be searched out in different areas of Britain – it is not fully comprehensive but it does contain over 500 suggestions which should cater for a variety of tastes. Where dates and times of opening are indicated, every precaution has been taken to ensure that the information is correct at the time of going to press, but it would be advisable to check with your contemplated venue before setting off.

It is hoped that this publication will serve to introduce its readers to hitherto unknown places of interest which they will look back upon later as having brought them a jolly good day out.

As there are practical limits to the distances which can be conveniently covered on short outings of this kind the book has been subdivided into geographical sections. This should bring the features of a given area within road or rail reach of most people living within its boundaries as well as some people in adjoining areas. These areas are shown on the map on page 6 – the numbers given relating to the appropriate chapters.

CONTENTS

INTRODUCTION

The increase in leisure time, which is rapidly becoming accepted as one of the most important benefits of modern times, has created a demand for suggestions as to the means by which to spend it. There are, of course, an infinite variety of attractions to choose from but this book is selective inasmuch as it is limited to the fourteen broad categories which follow.

AMUSEMENT PARKS. The whole family will enjoy visiting one or more of Britain's amusement parks which provide a mixture of thrilling rides, sports events, games and exhibitions. Many of the parks also include boating lakes and fairground sideshows, with everything to be enjoyed in the relaxed and carefree atmosphere for which they are so justly renowned.

BOAT EXCURSIONS. Britain's lakes and waterways offer a variety of contrasting scenery. The lochs of Scotland and the English lakes are in settings which provide the visitor with some truly spectacular natural beauty. Hundreds of rivers, broads and canals pass through interesting towns and pleasant countryside while the canals, in particular, can reveal a fascinating insight into our historic and industrial past.

CASTLES. The earliest castles were simple mounds or mottes, reinforced with timber and earth. These were usually dug from a ditch which formed the moat. The Normans introduced the massive stone castles to Britain. These heavily defended structures had enormously solid walls and the usual layout consisted of two adjacent courtyards, an outer and inner bailey. Inside the communal wall stood the keep, consisting of a huge tower with an entrance at first-floor level which made it easier to repel attackers.

During the reign of Edward I an ambitious building programme was undertaken. The heart of the fortress was no longer the keep. Outer walls were strengthened to become an integral part of the defence which included projecting towers. The gatehouses were heavily fortified and the outer part of the archway normally housed the portcullis. Elaborate approaches to the gatehouses were constructed with drawbridge mechanisms equipped with counterweights.

With the development of commerce arose the need to build town walls as a protection for the merchants, and later castles were used more as residences of the nobility than as fortifications. Existing castles were remodelled during the Renaissance and many of the castles were built in the Italian style. Following the Wars of the Roses, Henry VIII built a number of castles and forts around the shores of southern England.

Our selection includes a number of fascinating castles that are worth visiting in the British Isles. Many of the castles were built purely for defence. Some were subsequently fortified, whilst others were built as fortified dwellings. A comprehensive list of castles that are open to the public appears in *Historic Houses, Castles and Gardens*, published annually by ABC Travel Guides Limited.

CAVES. A visit to an underground cave will reveal an excitingly colourful subterranean world. Caves are one of the many wonders of nature and have been formed over millions of years, resulting in vast underground caverns and hollows. The strange beauty of the natural rock face manifests itself in a variety of subtle tints and textures. The ceaseless action of running water over millions of years has created come truly awe inspiring effects, of which the most remarkable are stalagmites and stalactites. Recent exploration of cave systems has exposed skeletons and relics of Paleolithic cavemen who once inhabited the caves as long as 10,000 years ago. Guided parties are allowed to see many of the cave systems.

PARKS AND GARDENS. The widespread interest in parks and gardens in the British Isles is reflected by the innumerable open spaces maintained by local authorities for the pleasure of the public and by the many magnificent privately-owned gardens which are also opened to the public at advertised times, either free or in return for a small contribution.

PLEASURE FLIGHTS. Most people taking an air flip have never flown before so the programme at most airports provides an introduction. The usual time in the air is ten minutes. With the excitement of take-off and landing, this allows enough time to appreciate the view, yet is not long enough to let the novelty wear off.

Passengers, who are usually slightly nervous, may prefer a twin-engined aircraft, such as the Aztec, although a single-engined aircraft has just as high a safety record. Similarly, with only ten minutes in the air, there is no time even to begin wondering about feeling air sick.

The types most likely to be encountered are the three-passenger seaters, such as Cessna 172 and Piper Cherokee or perhaps the larger, twin-engined Aztec carrying five passengers. The flight will probably reach a height of not more than 1,000 feet. Take-off and landing speeds may range between 70 and 90 mph, and speed while in the air is likely to be just over 100 mph.

SPAS AND HISTORIC CITIES. A surprisingly high proportion of Britain's towns and cities are of tremendous interest on account of their historical background, their literary associations, their architectural qualities or for the beauty of the setting in which they have developed. They can handsomely repay the attention that so many of them richly deserve, as those to which we now briefly refer will prove when you see them.

THE SEASIDE. Man has always been fascinated by the lure of the sea, but until the mid-19th century there was little to attract crowds of visitors to the coast. Sea bathing became fashionable earlier in that century among members of the gentry who had heard about the medicinal qualities of salt water and sea air and places like Scarborough, Brighton and Margate were becoming popular.

The advent of railways opened the seaside to the great mass of the population. The Victorians adored the seaside and frequently organised day excursions and family outings. The different resorts faced fierce competition and built piers, hotels, music halls and amusement parks.

The Edwardians were responsible for the bawdy good humour which is still very much a part of the seaside. Theatres and vibrant music halls became permanent fixtures, in addition to the ever-popular Punch and Judy, buckets and spades, and donkey rides across the sand.

Today's generation is still attracted by the invigorating atmosphere of the seaside. Things have certainly changed, and although the music hall has been replaced by bingo, some of the piers have been destroyed and the beaches have become even more crowded, the seaside is still essentially the same as it was 100 years ago. There is nothing quite like relaxing on the sand or idling the time away by watching the ships sail past.

Our selection includes a number of the best coastal resorts in Britain and lists some of the amenities and places of interest.

ZOOS. Educational and enjoyable, zoos can teach us a great deal about the behavioural pattern of animals. Zoos also play a leading role in the conservation of an increasing number of species that are threatened by extinction. Man has learned that animals, like humans, cannot be happy incarcerated in confined quarters and greater emphasis is now placed on the building of attractive enclosures which simulate the animal's natural environment. This has led to the introduction of animal safari parks through which it is possible to drive, provided, of course, that car doors and windows are kept securely closed.

There are about 80 zoos, safari parks and specialised animal collections in the United Kingdom, attracting 15 million visitors each year. A complete list of zoos is published in *Guide to British Zoos* by Geoffrey Schomberg, Penguin Books Ltd.

COUNTRY HOUSES. The constant threat of skirmishes and raids by feudal neighbours meant that the homes of the nobles had to be fortified. The earlier dwellings were constructed of wood and thatch but these were easily destroyed by fire. The homes of the more wealthy landowners, notably the church, were built with stone. Fortified manor houses included moats and drawbridges and many of them were designed to resemble castles, although considerations of comfort were made to weigh equally with those of defence.

It was during the 16th century that architecture blossomed to fruition, influenced by continental styles and craftsmen, highlighting an age of artistic and intellectual achievement. Grandiose residences such as Hampton Court and Burghley House were amongst the earlier Tudor masterpieces. During the 17th and 18th centuries great houses like Blenheim Palace and Castle Howard culminated the careers of such architects as Sir John Vanbrugh, Sir Christopher Wren and Inigo Jones. The arts flourished and an array of painters were commissioned by the aristocracy. The houses were luxuriously furnished and skilled craftsmen like Grinling Gibbons embellished the interiors with distinctive carvings. Formal and landscaped gardens were impressively laid out and one of the most famous exponents was "Capability" Brown.

We include a selection of interesting and historic country and stately homes which are open to the public. A comprehensive list of houses is found in *Historic Houses, Castles and Gardens*, published annually by ABC Travel Guides Ltd.

FACTORY TOURS AND CRAFT SHOPS. Factory tours are extremely popular and some manufacturers are inundated with requests from members of the general public. It is therefore essential to make adequate arrangements prior to the actual visit. Some companies restrict tours to those who have a special interest such as technicians, buyers or school leavers deciding upon a career. There are, however, a number of companies who welcome all visitors and the industries that they represent are highly diversified – anything from newspapers to distilleries. Our list contains an interesting selection of ideas for visits to factories and smaller craft workshops which employ local crafts and skills in the manufacture of their goods.

INNS AND COACHING HOUSES. During the height of the coaching era, inns were esteemed for the friendly and efficient service that they were able to provide. A major London terminal might have seen the dispatch of as many as eighty coaches a day. The most thriving inns radiated from London along the major routes, providing refreshment and overnight accommodation for the weary passengers.

Some of the earliest inns were church hostels and doss houses, usually within the precincts of a monastery or cathedral. Between 1800 and 1840, coach services and coaching houses enjoyed remarkable prosperity. Teams of six horses were changed every 10 or 15 miles. This prosperity came to a sudden end with the development of the railways. Some of the more astute coaching tycoons were able to sell out at a profit and invest their money in the new railway companies.

The advent of the motor car renewed the popularity of inns and perhaps one of the most delightful instances of the fusion of the two eras could be seen in a notice quite often displayed at the beginning of this century. "Stabling for motor cars. Engineers in attendance."

LIGHT RAILWAYS. Steam has disappeared from our main line railways but important relics of the golden age of steam live on through the efforts of enthusiasts who have been instrumental, through Preservation Societies and private enterprises, in restoring a growing number of narrow and standard gauge lines in many different parts of Britain. Between them they are carrying ever-increasing numbers of appreciative and enthusiastic passengers through some of the loveliest scenery in the world.

MUSEUMS. Most towns contain a museum that is open for the use of the general public. Many of the buildings that we have listed as *Castles* or *Country Houses* have their own museums, in addition to the works of art and furniture that are on show to the public. Our list also includes houses which have been associated with famous people, notably writers and men of action. A comprehensive list of museums is published in *Museums in Britain* by ABC Travel Guides Ltd.

AREA ONE

Northumberland, Durham, Cumberland, Westmorland, North Lancashire, North Yorkshire.

BOAT EXCURSIONS.

Derwentwater. Keswick. Derwentwater Launch Co., 13 Helvellyn Street, Keswick, Cumberland, CA12 4EN. (Keswick 72263 and 72982.) Lake trip. Economic party charter, minimum 10, maximum 400. Commentator available on advance notice. Frequent daily service Easter – October. Keswick 10 mins; Ashness Gate 10 mins; Lodore 10 mins; High Brandlehow 10 mins., Low Brandlehow 10 mins., Hawse End.

Lake Windermere. Bowness Bay Boating Co., Bowness-on-Windermere, Westmorland. (Windermere 3360.) Economic party charter minimum 12, maximum 500. Frequent daily service Easter – October. Bowness 2 hours lakeside return cruise. Bowness 1½ hours, Ambleside and island return cruise.

CASTLES

Alnwick Castle, *The Duke of Northumberland.* Seat of the Percy family since Norman times. Keep, armoury, guard chamber, library and other apartments. Dungeons, early British and Roman museum. Open daily except Fri. May – September, 13.00 – 16.30. Alnwick, Northumberland.

Bamburgh Castle. *Lord Armstrong.* A restored Norman castle with a fine keep. Open daily Easter – September, 10.00 – 20.00. 16 miles north of Alnwick, Northumberland.

Muncaster Castle. *Sir William Pennington-Ramsden.* Family seat since 13th century. Notable furniture, china, carpets, silver, paintings and library. Gardens with rhododendrons and azaleas, bird gardens, deer, bears, garden

Lake Windermere
from Bowness

centre. Refreshments. Open Wed., Thu., Sat., Sun. and Bank Holiday Mon., Easter – September. 14.00 – 17.00. Ravenglass, Cumberland CA18 1RQ. On A595.

Raby Castle. *Lord Barnard.* Large 14th century building with one tower reputed to date from 11th century. English, Dutch and Flemish paintings and fine period furniture. Associations with Charles I. Teas. Open Sun. and Bank Holiday Mon., Easter – September. Wed. and Sat., June – September. Mon., Tue. and Thu. in August, 14.00 – 17.00. 1 mile north of Staindrop, Durham, on A688.

CAVES

Stump Cross Cavern, Greenhow Hill, Pateley Bridge, Yorkshire HG3 5JL. (Clapham 242.) Trip lasts 25 mins. Party maximum 60. Open Sat. and Sun. Daily March – September, 10.00 – 18.00.
White Scar Cavern, Ingleton, near Carnforth, Yorkshire. (Ingleton 244.) Trip lasts 40 mins. Party maximum 30. Open Sun. Easter – October. Daily Easter – September. Other months by appointment. 10.00 – 18.00.

COUNTRY HOUSES

Castle Howard. *George Howard, Esq.* Designed by Sir John Vanbrugh, the house contains a collection of pictures, porcelain, tapestries, statuary and 17th century costumes. Rolling parkland with a lake, Temple of the Four Winds and Hawksmoor's circular mausoleum. Refreshments. Open daily, except Mon. and Fri., Easter – September, 13.30 – 17.00 and Bank Holiday Mon., 11.30 – 17.30. Malton, 14 miles north-east of York, off A64. (Coneysthorpe 333.)
Holker Hall. *Hugh Cavendish, Esq.* Largely rebuilt in 1873 with fine interior wood carvings. Park with Fallow and rare Formosan deer. Children's farm, play area and Lakeland craft centre. Refreshments. Open daily, except Sat., Easter to mid-October, 10.30 – 18.00. 4 miles south-west of Grange-over-Sands, Lancashire. (Flookburgh 328.)
Leighton Hall. *Major and Mrs. Reynolds.* An early 19th century neo-Gothic facade with fine furniture and pictures. The house is set in beautiful surroundings. Teas. Open Wed., Sun. and Bank Holiday Mon., May – September, 14.30 – 18.00. Carnforth, Lancashire, off A6. (Carnforth 2729.)
Levens Hall. *Mrs. O. R. Bagot.* A fine Tudor manor with topiary garden in the Le Nôtre style. Steam collection,

Alnwick Castle

garden centre. Refreshments. Open Sun. and Tue. – Thu., May – September 14.00 – 17.00. 5 miles south of Kendal, Westmorland, on A6. (Sedgwick 321.)
Newby Hall. *Major E. R. F. Compton.* An 18th century house with an Adam interior. Superb Gobelins tapestries and classical sculpture. 25 acres of gardens with miniature railway and river launch. Children's playground. Refreshments. Open Wed., Thu., Sat., Sun. and Bank Holiday Mon. and Tue., Easter – mid-October, 14.00 – 18.30. Skelton on Ure, 4 miles south-east of Ripon, Yorkshire, off B6265. (Boroughbridge 2583.)

FACTORY TOURS AND CRAFT SHOPS

Beer. Trip lasts 2 hours. No children under 14. Visits: Weekdays 14.30. Parties must give 2 weeks' notice. Party maximum number 20. Contact: Personnel Department, Scottish & Newcastle Breweries Ltd., PO Box 1 RA, The Tyne Brewery, Callowgate, Newcastle-upon-Tyne NE99 1RA. (Newcastle 25091.)
Cigarettes. Trip lasts 2 hours. No children under 12. Refreshments available. Visits: Mon. – Thu., 14.00. Parties must give 3 months' notice. Maximum party number 35. Contact: Public Relations Department, W. D. & H. O. Wills Ltd., New Coast Road, Newcastle-upon-Tyne NE7 7SJ. (Newcastle 665501.)

Engineering. Trip lasts 1½ hours. Visits: Mon. – Fri., 9.00 – 17.00. Parties must give 10 days' notice. Maximum party number 15. Contact: Training Officer, British Engines Ltd., St. Peter's, Newcastle-upon-Tyne 6. (Newcastle 659091.)

Newspapers. Trip lasts 1½ hours. Visits: Mon., Tue., Wed. and Thu., ,19.00. Parties must give 2 months' notice. Maximum party number 30. Contact: Publicity Department, Newcastle Chronicle & Journal Ltd., Thomson House, Great Market, Newcastle-upon-Tyne. (Newcastle 27500, ex 254.)

Soft Drinks. No children under 15. Trip lasts 2¼ hours. Visits: Tue. and Wed., 14.30. Parties must give 7 months' notice. Party maximum number 20. Contact: Personnel Officer, Beecham's Foods Ltd., Vicar's Lane, Newcastle-upon-Tyne. Newcastle (665401.)

The Dining Room, Holker Hall

Spinning. Travel rugs, scarves, tweeds. Open weekdays 9.00 – 17.00. Otterburn Mill Ltd., Otterburn, Newcastle-upon-Tyne.

Tea merchandising. Trip lasts 2 hours. Visits: Tue., Wed. and Thu., 14.00. Parties must give advance notice. Maximum party number 36. Contact: Ring-

tons Ltd., Algernon Road, Newcastle-upon-Tyne NE6 2YN. (Newcastle 656181.)

Weaving. Fine worsted cloth. Open: Daily 9.00 – 18.00. Grewelthorpe Handweavers, Grewelthorpe, Ripon, Yorkshire. (Kirkby Malzeard 209.)

Weaving. Exclusive colours and designs, mohair rugs, scarves and stoles. Open daily 9.00 – 17.00. Chris Reekie, Old Coach House, Grasmere, Westmorland. (Grasmere 221.)

Woodcraft. Table lamps, book ends, stools, carved leaf dishes. Open daily 8.00 – 20.00. Acorn Industries, Brandsby, York. (Brandsby 217.)

INNS AND COACHING HOUSES

George Hotel (A591 and 594), St. John's Street, Keswick, Cumberland (0596-72076). A coaching inn dating from 16th century. Speciality: Spiced chicken George. Free house. Parking at rear of building. Coach parties of up to 70 welcome for lunch only.

Golden Lion (A167, 168 & 684), Market Place, Northallerton, Yorkshire (Northallerton 2404). An old posting house on the London to Edinburgh road. Dances held weekly in winter. Free house. Coach parties up to 40 welcome.

Royal Oak (A66), Bongate, Appleby, Westmorland (Appleby 51463). A coaching house dating back to the 14th century, it has been considerably extended and modernised. Free house. Coach parties welcome.

The Swan (A591), Grasmere, Westmorland (Grasmere 223). 300 years old and mentioned by Wordsworth: "Who does not know the famous Swan", and patronised by Sir Walter Scott. It has a pleasant garden and, surprising for a public house, keeps its own herd of cows to provide milk that is really fresh. Speciality: Steak Pauline. Free house.

Salutation Hotel (A591 and 593), Lake Road, Ambleside, Westmorland (Ambleside 2244). It was established as a hostelry in 1656 and became a leading coaching inn. There are fine views. Specialities: Tournedos flambé à la champagne and les goujons à volaille gourmet. Coach parties welcome.

LIGHT RAILWAYS

Ravenglass, Cumberland – Dalegarth. 35 minutes each way. Service all year, weekdays twice daily, also April – November weekends. Refreshments. Economic party charter minimum 20, maximum 600. Ravenglass & Eskdale Railway. Telephone Ravenglass 226.

MUSEUMS

Bowes Museum. *Durham County Council.* A wide range of artistic and beautiful objects from Europe from medieval to 19th century periods. Refreshments. Open daily 10.00 – 17.30. Sun. from 14.00 – 17.00. November – March until 16.00. Barnard Castle, 16 miles west of Darlington, off A67.

Hill Top. *The National Trust.* The 17th century house where Beatrix Potter wrote the Peter Rabbit books. The house contains her furniture, china, pictures and some of her original drawings. Open daily Easter – September, 10.30 – 18.00. Sun. from 14.00. Near Sawrey, Lancashire.

Museum of Science & Engineering. A comprehensive collection of mining machinery, ships, marine engines, locomotives and models. Open daily 10.00 – 18.00. Tue and Thu. until 20.00. Sun. 14.30 – 17.30. Winter until 16.30. Sun. from 13.30 – 16.30. Exhibition Park, Great North Road, Newcastle-upon-Tyne.

Wordsworth House. *The National Trust.* The 18th century house where William Wordsworth was born. Open daily, except Fri. and Sun. Easter – September 10.30 – 12.30 and 14.00 – 16.30. Cockermouth, Cumberland.

Bowes Museum

PARKS AND GARDENS

Muncaster Castle, Cumberland. Rhododendrons mid-May – June. Also exotic birds, bears. Castle open Wed., Thu., Sat and Sun. Refreshments. Open daily April – September 13.00 – 18.00.

HISTORIC CITIES

Durham. Durham is one of the most visually exciting cities in Britain with its castle and magnificent Norman cathedral, towering loftily above the river Wear. Churches: The Cathedral; St. Margaret; St. Giles; St. Nicholas. Museum: Gulbenkian Museum of Oriental Art and Archaeology. Historical buildings: The Castle; St. Giles' Cottages; Kepier Hospital; The Bailey; Maiden's Castle; Bishop Cosin's Almshouses.

THE SEASIDE

Grange-over-Sands. Seaside attractions: Putting greens, open-air bathing pool, putting, bowls, tennis, archery, badminton, cinema. Children's amusements: Paddling pool. Items of interest: Cartmel Priory; Hampsfell Hospice

view point; ornamental and promenade gardens; Holker Hall and deer park.

Scarborough. Seaside attractions: Marineland amusement park, band, two cinemas, three theatres, water skiing, two outdoor and one indoor swimming pools, miniature golf and golf

The Cathedral, Durham

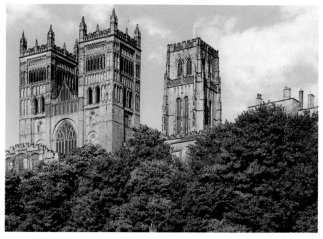

16

maze, two golf courses, putting greens, planetarium, tree walk, zoo. Working model of naval battles, Peasholm Lake Mon. and Thu. Sea trips from Lighthouse Pier. Continental festivals in June; Cricket festival in September. Children's amusements: Sands, kiddies' corner, adventure playground, trampolines, paddle boats and yacht pool, donkey rides, Treasure Island, water chute, miniature railway, fun house, Scalby Mills amusements. Live shows: Summer show: Floral Hall, Futurist and Spa Theatre. Concerts: Spa Theatre and Open-Air Theatre. Plays: Library Theatre. Dancing: Spa Ballroom and eleven night clubs and discotheques. Places of interest: Harbour; Lighthouse; Wood End Natural History Museum; Scarborough Museum; St. Thomas's Museum of local history; The Art Gallery; Fisherman's Craft Centre; King Richard III House; The Castle.

Whitby. Seaside attractions: Promenade pier, cinema, theatre, miniature golf and putting, bathing pool. Children's amusements: Sands, pony and donkey rides, boating lake, miniature railway. Live shows: Straight plays: Spa Theatre. Dancing: Floral Pavilion. Places of interest: 7th century Abbey ruins; 12th century Church; Fish harbour and auction; Captain Cook's house; Sandsend Bay.

ZOOS

Flamingo Park Zoo, Kirby Misperton, Yorkshire (Kirby Misperton 287). Lions and tigers fed 15.15, sealions 15.45, penguins at 16.15, elephants 16.30. Dolphin shows hourly from 13.00. Visitors may feed the animals. Fairground amusements, jungle cruise. Licensed catering seating 1,000. Open daily 10.00 – dusk. 2½ miles south of Pickering, off A169.

The Harbour, Whitby

Spa Bridge and South Bay, Scarborough

AREA TWO

South Lancashire, South Yorkshire, Derbyshire, Nottinghamshire, Lincolnshire, Cheshire.

AMUSEMENT PARKS

Belle Vue Park, Manchester 12. (061-223 1331.) Fairground amusements, waxworks, speedway and stock car stadium, ten-pin bowling, model village, sports stadium, wrestling, zoo. Licensed catering seating 2,000. Open daily 10.00 – dusk.

Sewerby Park, Bridlington, Yorkshire. (Bridlington 3769.) Set in the 50-acre grounds of a Georgian mansion. Pony rides, zoo, old English walled garden, golf course, archery, bowls, croquet, putting, children's corner. Refreshments, seating 100. Open daily 9.00 – dusk.

Licensed. Refreshments. Frequent afternoon service except Mon., Wed. evenings. April – September. New Brighton, round trip, 2 hours.

CASTLES

Ripley Castle. *Major Sir Joslan Ingilby, Bart.* The castle has been the home of the Ingilby family for 600 years. 15th century gatehouse, Tudor armoury, Adam living quarters. Grounds laid out by "Capability" Brown. Teas. Open Sun. and Bank Holiday Mon., May – September, 14.00

The Castle Gateway, Skipton

BOAT EXCURSIONS

Dee. Bithell's Boats Ltd., 2 Souters Lane, Chester. (Chester 25394.) Economic party charter, minimum 30, maximum 400. Frequent daily service Easter – October, 10.00 – 19.00. Chester return trip ¾ hour.

Mersey. MPTE, Sea View Road, Wallasey, Lancashire. (051-639 6021.) Economic party charter, maximum 600.

– 18.00. Ripley, Yorkshire, 3½ miles north of Harrogate.

Skipton Castle. Site fortified shortly after the Conquest. Edward I stayed there in 1292. Drum towers were added in 1307. Withstood a three-year siege in the Civil War and was restored in 1659. Open daily, 10.00 – 19.00 (or dusk). Sun. from 14.00. Skipton, Yorkshire.

Great Rutland
Cavern, Heights of
Abraham

Sewerby Park,
Bridlington

CAVES

Blue John Caverns, Castleton, Derbyshire. (Hope 638.) Trip lasts 45 mins. Open daily 10.00 – 18.00 (or dusk).
Great Rutland Cavern, Heights of Abraham, Derbyshire. (Matlock Bath 2365.) Trip lasts 20 mins. Open daily Easter – September, 10.00 – 18.00.

Great Masson Cavern, Heights of Abraham, Derbyshire. (Matlock Bath 2365.) Open daily August and summer Bank Holiday, 11.00 – 18.00.
Ingleborough Cavern, Clapham, Yorkshire. (Clapham 242.) Trip lasts 40 mins. Party maximum 60. Open Sat. and Sun. all year. Mon. – Thu., mid-March – October, 10.30 – 18.00.
Peak Cavern, Castleton, Derbyshire. (Hope 285.) Trip lasts 45 mins. Party maximum 80. Open daily Easter to mid-September, 10.00 – 18.00.
Speedwell Cavern, Castleton, Derbyshire. (Hope 512.) Includes a subterranean boat trip. Trip lasts 35 min. Boat capacity 20. Open daily, 10.00 – 18.00.
Treak Cliff Cavern, Castleton, Derbyshire. (Hope 571.) Trip lasts 30 mins. Refreshments, seating 100. Open daily, 10.00 – 18.00.

COUNTRY HOUSES

Browsholme Hall. *Col. Robert Parker.* A Tudor mansion with Elizabethan and Stuart panelling, china, tapestries, furniture and pictures. Landscaped grounds. Open Thu., Sat., Sun. and Bank Holiday Mon., Easter to mid-October, 14.00 – 18.30. 3½ miles north-west of Clitheroe off B6243. (Stonyhurst 330.)
Burton Agnes Hall. *Marcus Wickham Boynton, Esq.* A fine Elizabethan house with carved ceilings and overmantles, antique furniture and modern paintings. Refreshments. Open daily May – mid-October, 13.45 – 17.00. Sun. until 18.00. Burton Agnes, 6 miles south-west of Bridlington, Yorkshire, on A166. (Burton Agnes 324.)
Burton Constable. *J. R. Chichester-Constable, Esq.* Elizabethan house with some 18th century state rooms by Adam, Wyatt and Carr. Parkland and lakes landscaped by "Capability" Brown. Refreshments. Open Sat. and Sun., Easter – September. Tue., Wed. and Thu., Whitsun – September and Bank Holiday Mon., 12.00 – 18.00. Burton Constable, 7½ miles north-east of Hull, Yorkshire, on A165. (Skirlaugh 400.)
Capesthorne. *Lt. Col. Sir Walter Bromley-Davenport.* An 18th century building containing a collection of pictures, Greek vases, marbles, furniture and silver. Refreshments. Open Sun. and Bank Holiday Mon., April – September. Wed. and Sat., May – September, 14.00 – 17.30. Sat. until 16.00. 7 miles south of Wilmslow, Cheshire, off A34. (Chelford 221.)
Gawsworth Hall. *D. Raymond Richards, Esq.* A 15th century half-timbered manor house. Former home of Mary Fitton,

supposedly the dark lady of Shake-speare's sonnets. Refreshments. Open daily April – October, 14.00 – 18.00. 3 miles south of Macclesfield, Cheshire, on A536. (North Rode 456.)

Haddon Hall. *The Duke of Rutland.* A famous medieval manor set in a terraced rose garden. Refreshments. Open daily, except Sun. and Mon., April – September, 11.00 – 18.00. 2 miles south-east of Bakewell, Derbyshire, A6. (Bakewell 2855.)

Harewood House. *The Earl of Harewood.* A John Carr and Robert Adam building, furnished by Thomas Chippendale. The house contains a collection of fine china, silver and paintings. Formal gardens and parkland by "Capability" Brown. Tropical bird garden. Refreshments. Open daily, Easter – September, 11.00 – 18.00. The bird garden is only open at week-ends during the winter. 7 miles south of Harrogate, Yorkshire, off A61. (Harewood 331 and 225.)

Kedleston Hall. *The Viscount Scarsdale.* A fine original Adam house with magnificent hall and State rooms. Collection of Indian silver and ivories. Open Sun., also Bank Holiday Mon., May – September, 14.00 – 18.00. 4½ miles north-west of Derby, off A6. (Derby 840386.)

Melbourne Hall. *The Marquess of Lothian.* A beautiful collection of pictures, furniture and works of art. Gardens in the style of Le Nôtre. Wrought iron birdcage by Bakewell. Open Sun., Easter – October. Tue. – Thu. and Sat., July – September, 14.00 – 18.00. Melbourne, 8 miles south of Derby, off A514. (Melbourne 2502.)

Oakes Park. *Major and Mrs. T. Bagshawe.* A Restoration house altered during the 18th and 19th centuries containing tapestries and paintings. Refreshments. Open Sat., Sun. and Bank Holiday Mon. and Tue. from mid-May until mid-September, 14.00 – 18.00. Norton, 4 miles south of Sheffield, on B6054. (Sheffield 746468.)

Sledmere House. *Sir Richard Sykes, Bart.* A Georgian house containing some fine plasterwork by Joseph Rose. Chippendale, Sheraton and French furniture, porcelain and antique statuary. Park and gardens. Refreshments. Open Sun. and Bank Holiday Mon., Easter – September. Daily, except Mon. and Fri., mid-May – September, 13.30 – 17.30. Driffield, 24 miles east of York, off B1251.

Tatton Park. *The National Trust.* Built by Samuel Wyatt, the house contains an interesting collection of furniture and 2,000 acres of parkland. Refreshments. Open daily, except Mon., April – mid-October, 14.00 – 17.45. 3½ miles north of Knutsford, Cheshire, on A5034. (Knutsford 3155.)

Thoresby Hall. *The Countess Manvers.* An exceptional Victorian mansion with State apartments and a Great Hall. The house is situated in Sherwood Forest. Open Wed., Thu., Sat., Sun. and Bank Holidays, mid-April – September, 14.30 – 18.00. 4 miles north of Ollerton, Nottinghamshire, off A614.

The George Hotel, Stamford

Wilberforce House. *Hull Corporation.* A fine 17th century mansion, birthplace, in 1759, of William Wilberforce. Rooms are furnished in styles ranging from Elizabethan to Victorian, with personal relics and documents of Wilberforce's campaign for the abolition of slavery. Open daily, except Christmas and Good Friday, 10.00 – 17.00. Sun. 14.30 – 16.30. 25 High Street, Hull, Yorkshire. (Hull 27625.)

FACTORY TOURS AND CRAFT SHOPS

Cabinet Making. Furniture, restoration and wood turning. Open any reasonable time by appointment. Peter Davis, The Woodcraft Shop, Endwood Cottage, Tetford, Horncastle, Lincolnshire. (Tetford 228.)

Ironwork. Hand-forged gates, grilles, dog grates, light fittings and balustrades. Open weekdays 9.00 – 17.30, weekends by appointment. Gerald Kershaw, Bent House Farm, Oldfield, Oakworth, near Keighley, Yorkshire. (Haworth 3689.)

Jewellery. Coloured ceramic stones set in hand-beaten pewter rings, earclips, brooches, pendants and cuff links. Open weekdays 9.00 – 17.00, by appointment. Margaret Jones, West End, Gt. Eccleston, near Preston, Lancashire. (Gt. Eccleston 70319.)

Newspapers. Trip lasts 2 hours. No children under 14. Visits: Mon. – Fri., 13.30. Parties must give 2 weeks' notice. Maximum party number 15. Contact: Manchester Evening News, 164 Deansgate, Manchester M60 2RD. (061-832 7200, ex 566.)

Newspapers. Trip lasts 2½ hours. No children under 14. Visits: Mon. – Fri., except Thu., 20.30. Parties must give 2 weeks' notice. Maximum party number 15. Contact: Manchester Guardian, 164 Deansgate, Manchester M60 2RD. (061-832 7200, ex 566.)

Porcelain. Trip lasts 1¼ hours. No children under 11. Catering facilities available. Visits: Mon. – Thu., 14.30. Parties must give 1 year's notice. Maximum party number 30. Contact: Royal Crown Derby Porcelain Co. Ltd., Osmaston Road, Derby DE3 8JZ. (Derby 47051.)

Pottery. Domestic stoneware and ceramic sculpture. Also limited editions of litho poster poems. Open any reasonable time by appointment. Haworth Pottery, 27 Main Street, Haworth, near Keighley, Yorkshire. (Haworth 3877.)

Pottery. Earthenware and stoneware, also ceramic sculptures and figures. Open any reasonable time by appointment. The Lunesdale Pottery, Farriers Yard, Caton, near Lancaster. (Caton 770284.)

Pottery. Hand-thrown pottery and earthenware coffee sets, jars, beakers, dishes and jewellery. Open daily 9.30 – 17.30. Pru Green, Alvingham Pottery, Alvingham, Louth, Lincolnshire. (South Cockerington 230.)

Shellcraft. Shells for flower arrangements and collections, Abalome jewellery, shell animals, pendants, bracelets, dress rings and driftwood sculptures. Open weekdays 10.00 – 16.00, except Thu. Shellcraft, Mary's Cottage, Vicarage Lane, Frodsham, Cheshire WA6 7DX. (Frodsham 33375.)

Silverware and jewellery in modern designs. Open any reasonable time by appointment. Brian Asquith, Turret House, Youlgreave, Bakewell, Derbyshire. (Youlgreave 204.)

Weaving. Handwoven floor rugs, knee rugs, shoulder bags, cushion covers, table mats, pram covers and curtaining material. Open any reasonable time by appointment. Noelle M. Bose, Westoby, West End, Winteringham, near Scunthorpe, Lincolnshire DN15 9NS. (Winterton 729.)

Woodcarving. Birds, fishes, torsos, spoons, madonnas. Open all week by appointment. Michael Simpson, Windrush, East Keal, Spilsby, Lincolnshire. (Spilsby 3557.)

INNS AND COACHING HOUSES

Angel and Royal (A1, 52 and 607), High Street, Grantham, Lincolnshire (Grantham 5816). One of the oldest inns in Britain, the foundations date back to the 13th century when it was a hostel of the Knights Templar. The existing building was restored in the 15th century. The religious motif remains in the Pelican in Piety over the window in the bar. The dining room is the former state room were King John spent the night and Richard III signed the death warrant of the Duke of Buckingham. Charles I is also supposed to have stayed there and Edward VII quite definitely so, for it was he who granted the royal suffix. Specialities: Chef's chicken liver paté, crispy roast duckling with a sweet and sour sauce, lemon supreme made to an old fashioned recipe. Medieval banquets held regularly. Free house. Coach parties up to 40 welcome.

Bear and Billet (A41, 51 and 56), Lower Bridge Street, Chester. (Chester 21272). Formerly the town house of the Earl of Shrewsbury. Built in 1644 it has a magnificent four-storey black and white facade with remarkably handsome windows for the 17th century, incorporating as many panes of glass as the date of its construction. Free house. Parking at Roodee. Coach parties of up to 50 welcome.

Black Swan Peasholme Green, York (York 25236). A fine black and white half-timbered building dating from the 15th century. Almost certainly the birthplace of General Wolfe. Specialities: Spit roast beef cooked over an apple log fire. Coach parties up to 50 welcome.

Coach & Horses (A515), Fenny Bentley, near Ashbourne, Derbyshire (Thorpe Cloud 246). Reputed to date back to 15th century. A wealth of copper and brass against a background of old beams. Lawn garden with children's play area with slides and swings. Grill room, grillettes, garnished sandwiches. Parking on premises. Coach parties of up to 40 welcome.

The George (A1, 16, 43 and 606), St. Martin's, Stamford, Lincolnshire (Stamford 2101). Main block of the building was erected in 1597 by Lord Burghley, High Treasurer to Queen Elizabeth I, and his coat of arms is over the front door. Surviving from the coaching days is the room on the left of the entrance labelled London, for up travellers, and one on the right, called York, both richly panelled. Charles I stayed twice and William III once. A favourite stopping place of Sir Walter Scott.

The Parsonage, Haworth

Specialities: Roast sirloin of English beef served from the carving. Parking at rear of hotel. Free house.

The White Hart (Off A1, on A620 and 638), The Square, Retford, Nottinghamshire (Retford 3671). One of the old coaching inns, situated half way between London and Newcastle, first licensed in 1704 and supposed to be haunted. Free house.

LIGHT RAILWAYS

Grimsby – Humbertston. 20 minutes each way. Steam and diesel narrow gauge. Service: Frequent daily, Whitsun – October. Steam trains most Sundays.

The Old Bridge, Ilkley

The Clock Tower, Ripon

Lincolnshire Coast Light Railway, North Sea Lane, Humberston, Grimsby, Lincolnshire.

Keighley – Oxenhope. 70 minutes each way. Service: Saturday, Sunday and Bank Holiday Monday, all year Wednesday, June – August. Economic party charter minimum 45, maximum 600. Keighley & Haworth Valley Light Railway, Haworth Station, Keighley, Yorkshire. Telephone: Haworth 3629.

MUSEUMS

Bolling Hall Museum. A 15th century house with local period rooms and other house interiors, fully furnished and ranging up to the 19th century. Open daily 10.00 – 19.00. October – March 17.00. May – August 20.00. Bolling Hall Road, Bradford, Yorkshire.

Brontë Parsonage Museum. *The Brontë Society*. The home of the Brontë sisters with a collection of relics and some of their manuscripts. Open daily 11.00 – 18.00. October – March until 17.00. Sun. from 14.00. Haworth, 4 miles south-west of Keighley, Yorkshire.

Leeds City Art Gallery. A fine collection of English water colour artists, 17th and 18th century Italian, British and French paintings, modern paintings and sculpture. Open daily 10.30 – 18.30. Sun. 14.30 – 17.00.

Manchester Gallery of English Costume. Over a thousand dresses and two thousand accessories from the 17th century up to today, exhibited in a Georgian house. Open daily 10.00 – 20.00. Sun. from 14.00.

23

Railway Museum. A unique collection of historical locos, coaches, equipment, models and prints. Open daily June – August 10.00 – 17.00. Weekdays April, May, September and October. Queen Street, York.

West Yorkshire Folk Museum. A 15th century house and 17th century barn containing craft workshops which show West Yorkshire agricultural implements and coach and horse equipment. Open daily April – September 11.00 – 19.00. October – March until 17.00. Suns. in February, March, October and November. Halifax, A58.

GARDENS

Harlow Hill Gardens. Northern Horticultural Society gardens. Trials of selected ranges of flowers and vegetables. Refreshments. Open daily all year, 9.00 – sunset. $1\frac{1}{2}$ miles from Harrogate, Yorkshire.

PLEASURE FLIGHTS

Blackpool Airport. Air Navigation & Trading Co. Ltd. (Blackpool 45396). Flights all year. Licensed restaurant. Round Blackpool Tower, longer flights to Windermere and Southport available.

Manchester Airport. Airviews Ltd. Flights, including evenings, on weekdays only. Licensed restaurant.

The Rows, Chester

The Town Hall, Lancaster

24

The Guildhall
from Lendal Bridge,
York

SPAS AND HISTORIC CITIES

Chester. The former Roman city of Deva, today's city of Chester has many historic buildings and relics. Church: The Cathedral. Museums: King Charles Tower and Water Tower; Castle Grosvenor Museum. Buildings of interest: Leche House; Bishop Lloyd's House; Old Kings Head Hotel; Bear & Billet Inn; Pied Bull Hotel; City Walls; Watergate Street. Gardens: The Roodee; Grosvenor Park; The Groves; The Meadows; Water Tower Gardens. River trips from The Groves. Chester Zoo.

Harrogate. Originally famous for its mineral waters, Harrogate is now an important conference and holiday centre on the fringe of the Yorkshire moors. Church: St. Wilfrid's. Places of interest: Royal Pump Room Museum; Royal Hall; Grand Opera House; Valley Gardens.

Lancaster. Lancaster, on the river Lune, has played a leading part in British history and contains a number of interesting buildings. Churches: The Catholic Cathedral; St. Mary's; Friends' Meeting House; Priory Church. Museums: Lancaster Museum; King's Own Regimental Museum. Places of interest: The Castle; Quayside Prom-

enade; Custom House. Park: Williamson Park.

Lincoln. Lincoln occupies a rugged hill and overlooks the river Witham. The city has had a colourful past and traces of Roman, Norman and Danish occupation are amongst the many historic possessions to be seen. Churches: The Cathedral; St. Swithin's; St. Mary-le-Wigford; St. Peter at Gowts; St. Benedict. Museums: City and County Museum; Usher Gallery; Tennyson Research Centre. Places of interest: The Castle; The Guildhall; The Jew's House and Steep Hill; the Green Dragon; The Cardinal's Hat; The White Friars' House; The High Bridge; Bishop's Palace; Winnowsty Lane and Potter Gate; Exchequer Gate and Stonebow. Parks: Monks Road Arboretum; Boultham Park and Hartsholme Park.

York. The fascinating walled city of York with its Minster, castle, museum and charming streets has long been a popular tourist centre. Churches: York Minster; All Saints. Museums: Castle Museum; Railway Museum; Yorkshire Museum; City Art Gallery. Places of interest: Guildhall; Merchant Adventurers' Hall; Merchant Taylors' Hall; St. Anthony's Hall; Treasurer's House; St. William's College; King's Manor; City Walls; Clifford's Tower; St. Mary's Abbey; Shambles. River trips from Lendal Bridge or Ouse Bridge.

'The Glory Hole'
High Bridge, Lincoln

Blackpool Tower

Cleethorpes. Seaside attractions: Zoo, aquarium, band, water ski-ing, promenade pier, open-air swimming pool, illuminations August – September, cinema. Children's amusements: Sand, kiddies' corner, Punch & Judy, donkey and pony rides with traps, boating and paddling pools, miniature railway. Live shows: Summer show at pier Pavilion. Dancing at the Winter Gardens.

The Harbour
Bridlington

THE SEASIDE

Blackpool. Seaside attractions: Three amusement piers, Pleasure Beach, Golden Mile and Olympia amusement park. Tower zoo, aquarium and model village. 10 theatres, 9 cinemas. Illuminations September – October. Variety and revue at the Opera House, North, Central and South Piers. Circus at the Tower, ice show at the Ice Drome, dancing at the Tower and Winter Gardens (not Sun.). Children's amusements: Sand, kiddies' corner, Punch & Judy, donkey and pony rides, boating and paddling pools. Items of interest: Blackpool Tower ascent and views; Pleasure flights from Blackpool Airport; Stanley Park; Winter Gardens.

Bridlington. Attractions: Two promenade piers, two cinemas, two theatres, bingo, tennis, golf, zoo, miniature circus. Live shows: Revue at the Grand Pavilion. Dancing at the Spa Royal Hall (not Tue. and Sun.). Children's amusements: Sand, kiddies' corner, pony and donkey rides, boating pool, electric speedway, miniature railway. Items of interest: Flamborough Head lighthouse; Lifeboat house; Floral clock; Bayle Gate; Priory Church; Harbour; Sewerby Hall park and art gallery.

New Brighton. Seaside attractions: Promenade pier, New Palace amusement park, passing shipping, two cinemas, band, pleasure cruises on Royal Iris, two open-air bathing pools, crazy ·golf, bowls, cricket, trampolines, bathing beauty contests. Illuminations, June – October. Children's amusements: Sand, kiddies' corner, Punch & Judy, donkey and pony rides with traps, boating and paddling pool, miniature railway, trampolines. Live shows: Revue: Floral Pavilion; Summers how: Vale Park Arena. Dancing: Grosvenor, Riverside and Capitol Ballrooms and also several hotels.

Southport. Seaside attractions: Pier, Pleasureland amusement park, three cinemas, two theatres, model village, zoo, Birdville, aquarium, open-air sea-bathing lake and indoor baths, minia-ture golf and putting greens, Leisure centre, Go-karting, maze, canoes, water ski-ing demonstrations on the Marine Lake, Launch trips, pleasure flights from sands adjoining Pleasureland. Children's amusements: Clean sands, miniature railway, donkey and pony rides, model yacht and paddling pool, Peter Pan amusement park, trampolines. Live shows: Summer show: Floral Hall. Plays: Little Theatre. Dancing: Floral Hall, Marine Room, Dixieland Show-bar, Moulin Rouge and several clubs.

The Pier, Southport

Places of interest: Southport Bird Sanc-tuary; Museum; Art Gallery; Ainsdale Nature Reserve.

ZOOS

Belle Vue Zoo, Manchester 12 (061-223 1331). Big zoo park, aquarium and tropical river house. Also fairground amusements, speedway and stock car stadium, wrestling and ten-pin bowling. Visitors may feed some of the animals. Licensed catering seating 2,000. Open daily 10.00 – dusk. On A6.

Knaresborough Zoo, Conyngham Hall, Yorkshire (Knaresborough 2793). Nocturnal reptile and squirrel houses and talking birds. Sealions fed 12.00 and 15.15, animal handling demonstrations with lions, pumas, panthers and snakes. Refreshments. Open daily 10.00 – 19.00 April – October. 3 miles east of Harro-gate, off A59.

Natureland Marine Zoo, The Pro-menade, Skegness, Lincolnshire (Skeg-ness 4345). Specialises in rearing locally-born orphaned seal pups. Sealions fed at 10.00 and 15.00 and performing seals at 11.00, 12.00, 15.00 and 16.00. Pen-guins at 11.00 and 15.00. Reptile house, aquarium and Pets' Corner. Floral Palace of tropical plants including orchids, bananas, etc. Refreshments, seating 100. Open daily 10.00 – 19.30. winter to dusk.

North of England Zoological Society, Chester (Chester 20106). Animals exhibited in spacious outdoor enclosures. Tropical and nocturnal houses, reptile house, aquarium. Refreshments. Open daily 9.00 – dusk. 2 miles from Chester, off A41.

Marineland Oceanarium and Aquarium, Stone Jetty, Marine Road, Morecambe, Lancashire (Morecambe 4727). Performing dolphins, seals, sealions and also penguins and reptiles. Refreshments. Open 10.00 – 19.30, winter to 16.30.

Riber Castle Fauna Reserve & Wildlife Park, Riber Castle, Matlock, Derbyshire (Matlock 2073). Collection of British and European fauna, specialising in rare domesticated livestock and animal breeding so that many of the young can be seen in spring and summer. Model railway. Light refreshments, picnic area. Open daily 10.00 – 19.00. 2 miles from Matlock, off B6014.

Sherwood Zoo, Hucknall, Nottinghamshire (Hucknall 2425). Specialising in the "big cats". Aviary. Pony rides at weekends. Special foods provided for feeding. Refreshments. Reptile house, lions, leopards. Open daily Easter – October, 10.00 – 19.00. 7 miles north of Nottingham, on A611, M1 exit 26 and 27.

Southport Zoo, Princes Park, Southport, Lancashire (Southport 57434). Penguins, pelicans, lions, leopards, pumas, chimpanzees, etc., and parrot house. Pets corner with pony rides on summer afternoons. Refreshments, seating 50. Open daily 10.00 – dusk.

Winged World, Heysham Head, Lancashire (Heysham 52392). A large conservatory aviary housing a fine collection of softbilled birds. Indoor zoo. Licensed refreshments, seating 200. Open daily 10.00 – 19.30, winter to 17.00.

AREA THREE

North Wales, Shropshire, Staffordshire.

AMUSEMENT PARKS

Alton Towers, Alton, Staffordshire. (Oakamoor 449.) Extensive estate around the former home of the Earls of Shrewsbury. Fairground amusements, boating pool, scenic and aerial railways, conservatories, planetarium. Licensed catering seating 1,400. Open daily Easter to mid-October, 9.30 – 20.00.

Drayton Manor Park, near Tamworth, Staffordshire. (Tamworth 68481.) Amusements, boating, trains, chair lift and zoo all set in 160 acres of trees and water park. Licensed catering, party tearooms seating 1,100. Open daily Easter–October, 10.30 – 19.00.

CASTLES

Caernarvon Castle. Most important of the castles built by Edward I. Begun in 1283 with the enormous Eagle Tower. The polygonal towers and various coloured stones show Constantinople influence. Open daily May – September 9.30 – 19.00. March, April and October until 17.30. November – February until 16.00. Sun. October – March from 14.00.

Chirk Castle. *Lt. Col. Ririd and Lady Margaret Myddleton.* A 14th century border castle with 17th – 19th century furniture and decor. Associations with Thomas Seymour, Earl of Leicester and Charles I. Refreshments. Open Sun. and Bank Holiday Mon., Easter – September. Tue., Thu. and Sat., May – September 11.00 – 17.00. Wrexham, Denbighshire. 7 miles south of Llangollen, off A5.

Powis Castle. *The Earl of Powis.* Ancestral home of Powis family for over 500 years, containing fine plaster work, tapestry, paintings and furniture. Magnificent terraced gardens. Teas. Open Wed. – Sun., June – September, 14.00 – 18.00, Bank Holidays from 10.00. Welshpool, Montgomeryshire, off A483.

Caernarvon Castle,
Floodlit

Tamworth Castle. Norman walls and a tower surrounding a banqueting hall and State apartments with period furniture. Local history museum with early English coins. Open weekdays, 10.00 – 20.00 (or dusk). November – February, until 16.00 except Fri. Sun. from 14.00. Tamworth, Staffordshire.

COUNTRY HOUSES

Blithfield Hall. *Lady Bagot.* Elizabethan house containing a collection of Stuart relics, Georgian costumes and children's books and toys. Family coaches on display, garden centre and formal ground. Refreshments. Open Wed., Thu., Sat. and Sun., Easter – September. 14.30 – 18.00. Bank Holidays from 12.30 – 19.00. 4 miles north of Rugeley, Staffordshire, off B5013. (Dapplehead 249.)

Gwydir Castle. *Richard Clegg, Esq.* A Tudor mansion with parts dating back to the 13th century. Gardens with peacocks. Refreshments. Open daily, except Sat., Easter – October, 10.00 – 18.00. Near Llanrwst, Denbighshire.

Weston Park. *The Earl of Bradford.* A fine house of the Restoration period with collections of pictures, furniture, books and tapestries. Associations with Disraeli. Terraced gardens landscaped by "Capability" Brown. Woodland adventure playground, studio pottery, pets' corner, deer. Open daily, except Mon. and Fri., mid-April – September, 14.00 – 17.30, 4 miles north-east of Shifnal, Shropshire, on A5. (Weston-under-Lizard 207.)

Feathers Hotel, Ludlow

Alton Towers

FACTORY TOURS AND CRAFT SHOPS

Candles. Hand-made in paraffin wax and beeswax. Also wax sculptures. Open: Easter – September, daily 10.30 – 18.00, Sun. 14.00 – 17.00, October – December Mon. – Fri. 10.30 – 17.00. Celmi Candles, Cynfal House, Ffestiniog, Merionethshire. (Ffestiniog 675.)

Copperwork. Hand-worked jewellery, plates and trays, many depicting birds and animals. Open any reasonable time by appointment. Cernyw Copper, Plas Isa, Llangernyw, Abergele, Denbighshire. (Llanfair 202.)

Glass. Visits: Mon. – Fri., 10.30, 14.00, Fri. a.m. only. Appointment essential. Party maximum number 50. Contact: Visits Organiser, Royal Brierley Crystal, North Street, Brierley Hill, Staffordshire. (Brierley Hill 77054.)

Jewellery. Ceramic and baroque jewellery, tumbled and polished stones. Also a large selection of rocks, minerals and fossils. Open weekdays 9.00 – 17.00, Sat. and Sun. 12.00 – 16.00. Bwlchgwyn Crafts, Bwlchgwyn Quarry, near Wrexham, Denbighshire. (Coedpoeth 571.)

Metalwork. Silverplated and polished spun copper candelabra, goblets, cups and tankards. Open any reasonable time by appointment. C. J. Muller, Rhosian, Groeslon, Caernarvon. (Llanwanda 325.)

Pottery. Earthenware and stoneware. Animal studies, individual vases, bowls, with glazes from local materials. Open weekdays 11.00 – 21.00, Sat. 15.30 – 19.30. Bill & Olga Kinsman, Bryn Coch Pottery, Nebo, Penygroes, Caernarvonshire. (Penygroes 367.)

Snowdon Mountain Railway

Pottery. Individual pieces, ceramic sculptures, wall hangings. Open any reasonable time. Daphne Eales, Mawddach Pottery, Fairbourne, Merionethshire. (Fairbourne 530.)

Pottery. Trip lasts 2 hours. No children under 13. Visits: Mon. – Fri., 10.00 and 14.00, closed first two weeks in June and first week September. Parties must give 1 months' notice. Refreshments can be arranged. Maximum party number 20. Contact: Doulton Fine China Ltd., Nile Street, Burslem, Stoke-on-Trent, Staffordshire. (Stoke 84271.)

Pottery. Trip lasts 1¼ hours. No children under 12. Visits: Mon. – Fri., 10.00 and 14.00, closed last week June, first week July and first week September. Appointment essential. Maximum party number 40. Contact: Spode Ltd., Spode Works, Stoke-on-Trent, Staffordshire. (Stoke 48557.)

Pottery. Trip lasts 1 hour. Refreshments available. Visits: Mon. – Fri., 10.10, 11.35, 13.45 and 15.00 (Fri. not 15.00). Notice requested. Special arrangements necessary for parties of over 40. Refreshments available. Contact: Tours Hostess, Josiah Wedgwood & Sons Ltd., Barlaston, Stoke-on-Trent, Staffordshire. (Barlaston 2141.)

Sheepskin Goods. Rugs, coats, slippers, gloves, toys. Open weekdays 9.00 – 13.00 and 14.00 – 17.00. The Sheepskin Shop, The Old Mill Tannery, Tutbury, Burton-on-Trent, Staffordshire. (Tutbury 3300).

Slatework. Fireplaces, table lamps, wall lights, ashtrays, flower holders, house name plates. Open: Mon. – Fri. 8.30 – 17.00. W. A. Hawkes, Berwyn Slate Quarries, Horseshoe Pass, Llangollen, Denbighshire. (Llangollen 2302.)

Tapestry. Jacob's tweeds, made from natural coloured wool with traditional Welsh honeycomb bedcovers, tapestry tweed and tweed blankets and travel rugs. Open weekdays 9.30 – 17.00. Holywell Textile Mills Ltd., Greenfield Street, Holywell, Flintshire. (Holywell 2022.)

Wickerwork. Baskets of all sorts made to order. Also sun lounge furniture. Open daily by appointment only. James Johnson & Son, Station Road, Bangor-on-Dee near Wrexham, Denbighshire. (Bangor-on-Dee 417.)

Woodcarving. Welsh love spoons, animals, particularly horses, and shepherds' crooks. Wood lettering. Open: Mon. – Fri. 9.00 – 18.00, evenings and weekends by appointment. R. G. Jones, 57 Clwyd Avenue, Abergele, Denbighshire. (Abergele 3082.)

INNS AND COACHING HOUSES

Feathers Inn (A49, 41113 and 41117), Corve Street, Ludlow, Shropshire (Ludlow 2718). The beauty does not end with the highly timbered exterior of this inn built in 1521. Inside there is a wealth of panelling. In the lounge there is an antique iron back plate in the highly carved mantlepiece. More fine carving in other rooms. Speciality: Duck. Free house. Coach parties of up to 50 welcome.

The Lion (A5, 49, 458, 488 and 528), Wyle Cop, Shrewsbury (Shrewsbury 53107). Some rooms date from Tudor times but most from the 1770s when it was a celebrated coaching inn on the Holyhead road. The ballroom in Adam style was described by De Quincey and one of the bedrooms by Dickens, who both stayed there. So did Jenny Lind, Paganini and Disraeli, whose letter is displayed in the hotel. Traditional English fare. Free house. Coach parties up to 140 welcome.

LIGHT RAILWAYS

Llanberis – Mount Snowdon Peak. 2½ hours. Rack and pinion system. Open: April – October. Frequent services. Snowdon Mountain Railway, Caernarvonshire. Telephone: Llanberis 223

Llandudno – Great Orme. 20-minute service: Easter – October. Frequent daily services. Cable funicular in two stages, starting from Church Walks Station. Party maximum 48. Transport Officer, Great Orme Funicular, The Town Hall, Llandudno, Caernarvonshire. Telephone: Llandudno 77482.

Llanfair Caereinion. 40 minutes each way. Service: Sunday, Easter to mid-October. Saturday, Whitsun to mid-July and September to mid-October, 14.15 and 16.15. Weekdays mid-July–August, additionally at 11.00 mid-July – August. Economic party charter minimum 8, maximum 150. Welshpool & Llanfair Light Railway, Montgomeryshire. Telephone: Llanfair Caerinion 441.

Talyllyn Railway

Doctor Johnson's
House, Lichfield

of the Doctor and his contemporaries.
Open daily 10.30 – 13.00 and 14.00 –
17.00. November – March until 16.00.
Sun. from 14.30. Bread Street, Lichfield,
Staffordshire.

Stoke-on-Trent Museum. One of the
most important collections of pottery
with particular emphasis on English
Staffordshire. The museum also contains
a collection of local artistic works and
natural history. Open daily 10.00 –
18.00. Sun. from 14.30 – 17.00.

PARKS AND GARDENS

Alton Towers, Staffordshire. Extensive
estate around the former home of the
Earls of Shrewsbury with lawns and
woodland walks. Also fairground amusements. Refreshments. Open daily Easter
to mid-October, 9.30 – 20.00.

Portmadoc, Caernarvonshire. 44
minutes each way. Service: March –
December, frequently during April –
October. Buffet cars on all trains.
Economic party charter minimum 20.
Festiniog Railway, Harbour Station.
Telephone: Portmadoc 2384.

Towyn – Abergynolwyn. 45 minutes.
Daily, one week at Easter; April – May
September – October, one train daily,
Sunday, Tuesday, Wednesday and
Thursday. Daily mid-May to Sept –
ember.

Talyllyn Railway, Wharf Station,
Towyn, Merionethshire. Telephone:
Towyn 710472.

MUSEUMS

Arnold Bennett's House. The author's
early home with two rooms devoted to
his personal relics. Open Mon., Wed.,
Thu. and Sat., 14.00 – 17.00. 205
Waterloo Road, Cobridge, Stoke-on-
Trent, Staffordshire.

Izaac Walton's Cottage. The famous
angler's cottage, restored, together with
many mementos. Open daily, except
Tue., 10.00 – 12.00 and 14.30 – 16.30.
Shallowford, Staffordshire. 5 miles north-
west of Stafford, off A520.

Dr. Johnson's Birthplace. Rooms
containing relics, books and manuscripts

Pagoda Fountain,
Alton Towers

33

Bodnant Gardens (0492 6746). Rhododendrons, magnolias, camellias, terrace and water gardens. Open Tue., Wed., Thu., Sat. and Bank Holiday Mon., April – October, 13.30 – 16.45. 7 miles south of Colwyn Bay, Denbighshire.

Burford House Gardens. Some fine trees and shrubs and especially clematis, flowering June – September. Open daily May – September, 14.00 – 17.00. Tenbury Wells, 9 miles east of Ludlow, Shropshire.

Hodnet Hall Gardens. 60 acres of landscaped gardens with lakes and pools. Refreshments. Open daily April – September, 14.00 – 17.00. Sun. and Bank Holiday Mon. 12.00 – 18.30. Market Drayton, 12 miles north-east of Shrewsbury, Shropshire, off A53.

Portmeirion (Penrhyndeudraeth 228). Wild spring gardens, rhododendrons, azaleas and sub-tropical flora. Refreshments. Open daily all year, 10.00 – 18.00. 2 miles south-west of Penrhyndeudraeth, Merionethshire.

THE SEASIDE

Bangor. Seaside attractions: South amusement pier, bandstand Mon., Wed., Thu. and Sat. evening, cricket, tennis, golf, putting, bowls, football. Pixie

swimming pool. Launch trips by Laird's Boats from Marine Gardens and Sandy Scott from the Harbour. Central pier, lifeboat house. Illuminations: July – 1st

34

week September, switching-on time 22.30. Live shows: Variety, Little Theatre. Circus: Fossett's Circus, Castle Park. Dancing: Caproni's, Seacliffe Road and Milano's, Seacliffe Road. Two cinemas. Children's amusements: Sand, Kiddie Land, donkey and pony rides at Ballyholme Bay; Miniature train at South pier; Marine Gardens paddling pool. Items of interest: Cathedral; Abbey Parish Church, Newtonwards Road; Museum of Welsh Antiquities. Gardens: Castle Park; Marine Gardens; Stricklands Glen; Ward Park.

Llandudno. Seaside attractions: Amusement pier, two cinemas, three theatres, band, aquarium, three golf courses, steamer trips from the pier. Illuminations throughout the season. Children's amusements: Sands, kiddies' corner, Punch & Judy, donkey and pony rides, funfair, boating and paddling pool. Live shows: Variety: Pier Pavilion, Arcadia Theatre. Audience participation: Happy Valley. Straight plays: Grand Theatre. Dancing: Winter Gardens, Payne's Cafe Royal and various hotels. Places of interest: Lifeboat house; Rapallo House Museum; Great Orme Tramway; Great Orme Cabinlift.

ZOOS

Drayton Manor Park, near Tamworth, Staffordshire (Tamworth 68481). Zoo with tree and water park. Amusements. Licensed catering, party tea rooms seating 1,100. Open daily Easter – October, winter Sun. only 10.30 – 19.00. 2 miles south of Tamworth, on A4091.

Welsh Mountain Zoo, Flagstaff Gardens, Colwyn Bay, Denbighshire (Colwyn Bay 2938). Daily demonstrations of falconry at 15.00, weather permitting. Sealion feeding follows. Visitors can feed some of the animals. Licensed restaurant seating 100. Open daily, summer 10.00 – dusk, winter 11.00 – 16.00.

AREA FOUR

South Wales, Herefordshire, Worcestershire, Gloucestershire.

CASTLES

Cardiff Castle. Begun in 1090, most of the stonework was built in the 12th century with subsequent additions. Exotic interior decorations added in 1861. Refreshments. Open daily March – October, 10.00 – 12.00 and 14.00 – 16.00. May – September until 18.30, Sun. 14.00 – 17.00. City centre.

Berkeley Castle. *R. J. Berkeley, Esq.* Continuously inhabited for 800 years. Scene of murder of Edward II. Keep, dungeons, medieval kitchens, Great Hall and State apartments. Terraced gardens. Refreshments. Open Sun. April – October. Tue. – Sat., April – September, 14.00 – 17.30. Bank Holiday Mon. from 11.00. Sun. during October until 16.30. Berkeley, Gloucestershire. 15 miles south-west of Gloucester, off A38.

Sudeley Castle. *G. M. Dent-Brocklehurst, Esq.* Associations with Catherine Parr. Headquarters of Charles I during the Civil War. Fine pictures, tapestry and furniture. Teas. Open daily except Mon. from May – mid-October, 14.00 – 17.30. June – September, from 12.00. 6 miles north-east of Cheltenham, Gloucestershire, off A38.

CAVES

Dan-yr-Ogof Caves. Abercrave, Breconshire. (Abercrave 284.) Trip lasts 45 mins. Party maximum 25. Refreshments, seating 100. Open daily Easter – October 10.00 – 20.00.

Cardiff Castle

36

FACTORY TOURS
AND CRAFT SHOPS

Beer. Trip lasts 2 hours. No children under 16. Visits: Mon. – Thu., 10.30, 14.30 and 15.30. Parties must give 3 weeks' notice. Maximum party number 25. Contact: Courage (Western) Ltd., Victoria St., Bristol. (Bristol 294231, ex 30.)

The Cathedral
Bristol

Cider. Trip lasts 3 hours. No children under 14. Parties only. Visits: Mon. – Thu., morning and afternoon. Advance notice must be 8 months. Party maximum number 36. Contact: The Public Relations Officer, H. P. Bulmer Ltd., Ryelands Street, Hereford. (Hereford 6411.)

Cigarettes and Cigars. Trip lasts 2 hours. No children under 12. Teas available. Visits: Mon. – Fri., 10.00 and 14.00, Fri. mornings only. Parties must give 4 months' notice. Maximum party number 40. Contact: M.R., W. D. & H. O. Wills, Bedminster, Bristol BS99 7UJ. (Bristol 664641, ex 2254.)

Corn Dollies and cut straw work. Visitors welcome to try their hand with the easier plaits. Open most day times. Winifred Newton-Sealey, Perton Croft, Stoke Edith, Hereford.

Floral Pictures. Miniature to large, modern and period designs, also calendars, cards and arranged baskets. Straw decorative work. Open any time by appointment. Margaret Brown, Floralcraft, Wisteria Cottage, Old Grove, Westhide, Hereford. (Bartestree Cross 430.)

Furniture. Country-style rush-seated chairs, refectory tables, Welsh dressers and kitchen treen. Open weekdays 8.00 – 18.00. Hugh Loughborough, Panteg, Solva, Pembrokeshire. (Solva 294.)

Jewellery. In gold, silver, hand-cut gemstones. Open any reasonable time by appointment. Owen Swindale, 64 Worcester Road, Malvern, Worcestershire. (Malvern 61342.)

Leatherwork. Suede and leather work, clothing, bags, belts. Open weekdays 10.00 – 18.00, May – September till 17.30, Sun. from 14.00. Inskin, The Old Police Station, Main Street, Goodwick, Pembrokeshire. (Fishguard 2510.)

Stone. Stone and marble fireplaces, garden ornaments, carving and monuments. Open any reasonable time by appointment. John Hopkins & Son Ltd., The Stone Yard, Mill Street, Tewkesbury, Gloucestershire. (Tewkesbury 293170.)

Pottery. Cast, hand-thrown, stoneware tableware and ceramic sculpture. Open any reasonable time by appointment. Martin Homer, Workshop 20, 20 Church Street, Tenbury Wells, Worcestershire.

Pottery. Earthenware in original colours with traditional and modern designs. Open any reasonable time by appointment. Landshipping Pottery, Landshipping, Narberth, Pembrokeshire. (Martletwy 225.)

Pottery. Handmade plaques, sculptures, ceramic jewellery and tableware. Open weekdays 9.00 – 17.00. Sun. after 17.00 by appointment. Studio Pottery, Clyro, Hay-on-Wye, Breconshire. (Hay-on-Wye 510.)

Pottery. Hand decorated pottery. Open: Mon. – Fri. 9.00 – 18.00. June – September, Sat. and Sun. additionally. Dragon Pottery, East Street, Rhayader, Radnorshire. (Rhayader 318.)

Pottery. Hand-thrown pottery, domestic and individual items. Open weekdays 9.30 – 18.00. Campden Pottery & Craft Shop, Leasbourne, Chipping Campden, Gloucestershire.

Pottery. Tableware, individual pieces and stoneware, slab-built pots. Open daily 9.00 – 18.00. Helyg Pottery, Clay-pits, Ewenny, near Bridgend, Glamorganshire.

Pottery. Trip lasts 1 hour. No children under 5. Visits: Mon. – Fri., 10.00 – 11.45 and 14.00 – 15.45. Closed part of August. Parties must give advance notice. Maximum party number 40. Contact: The Curator, Worcester Royal Porcelain Co. Ltd., Severn Street, Worcester. (Worcester 23221, ex 41.)

Saddlery. Harness, soft leather goods, canvas work and trotting harness. Open weekdays 9.00 – 17.30. Peter Jones, 25 Cross Street, Abergavenny, Monmouthshire. (Abergavenny 2742.)

Wine. Bottling and merchandising. Trip lasts 2½ hours. No children under 18. Visits: Mon. – Fri., 14.30 and 18.30. Charge, including sherry tasting, 40p per head. Parties must give 19 months' notice. Maximum party number 40, minimum 24. Contact: John Harvey & Sons Ltd., 12 Denmark Street, Bristol. (Bristol 27661, ex 21.)

Woodwork. Traditional Welsh cradles and settees, egg racks, stools, coffee tables, cheese boards and turning of all kinds. Open weekdays, at any reasonable time, by appointment. P. E. Bossom, Clyn-y-Fran, Crymmych, Pembrokeshire. (Crymmych 347.)

Vale of Rheidol Railway

Tweeds. Trip lasts 1 hour. Visits: Mon. – Thur., 9.00 – 17.00, Fri. till 16.00. Parties must give 1 weeks' notice. Contact: The Manager, Cambrian Factory Ltd., Llanwrtyd Wells, Breconshire, LD5 4SD. (059 13211.)

Weaving, wool sorting, dyeing, carding, spinning, warping and winding by disabled persons. Open: Mon. – Fri., 8.15 – 17.00. Fri. till 15.45. Cambrian Factory Ltd., Llanwrtyd Wells, Breconshire LD5 4SD. (Llanwrtyd Wells 211.)

Woodworking. Turned woodware, particularly from burr oak. Standard lamps, salad and fruit bowls, egg cups, candlesticks. Also fabrics hand painted on premises, tray cloths, aprons, handkerchiefs. Open any reasonable time by appointment. G. J. Frude, Talarddu, Llanfaredd, Builth Wells, Breconshire.

Woollens. Visits: Mon. – Fri., 9.00 – 17.30. David Lewis & Sons Ltd., Rhydybont Mills, Llanybyther, Carmarthenshire. (Llanybyther 285.)

INNS AND COACHING HOUSES

Falcon Hotel (A44 and 465), Broad Street, Bromyard, Herefordshire (Bromyard 2408). While completely modernised, this inn, built in 1620, retains the historic atmosphere with genuine oak beams and, in the lounge, antique panelling. Free house. Parking at rear of building. Coach parties welcome, baliroom available.

Gloucester Flying Machine (Off M5), Green Street, Brockworth (Gloucester 66728). Named after the famous express coach. Maps and mementos from those days are to be seen in the lounge bar. Live music weekends, disco on Wednesdays. Free house. Coach parties up to 300 welcome.

Gupshill Manor (M5, A38 and 438), Gloucester Road, Tewkesbury, Gloucestershire GL20 5SY (Tewkesbury 292278). A fine timbered building embodying much of a 15th century mansion. Here Queen Margaret spent the night before the decisive battle of the Wars of the Roses and Bloody Meadow, where the Lancastrian army was routed, can be seen from the windows. Cuisine is largely Italian with Tournedos Rossini and scampi a la mode du chef. Ballroom available. Coach parties up to 160 welcome by appointment.

The Crown (A44 and 435), Market Place, Evesham, Worcestershire (Evesham 2404). In existence for 400 years, the hotel was originally built as a hostel for the abbey. A linking undergound passage can still be seen with the opening behind the reception desk. The fireplace in the main bar is also of antique interest. All food home grown and freshly cooked. Free house. Coach parties up to 120 welcome.

The Falcon (A46), Painswick, Gloucestershire (Painswick 2189). A 16th century inn with one of the oldest bowling greens in England. Specialities: Roast joints, game, casseroles. Parking at rear of premises. Coach parties welcome by appointment.

The New Inn (Off M5. On A38, 40 and 417), Northgate Street, Gloucester (Gloucester 22177). Built by Abbot Thokey in 1457 as a hostel for pilgrims to the shrine of the murdered Edward II at Winchcombe Abbey. It proved such a sound commercial venture that its early profits enabled the abbey to re-build the church as a cathedral. Fine galleried and stone flagged courtyard where the Queen's Players performed in 1559-60. Innumerable oak and chestnut beams. A Berni Inn. Free house. Three car parks within 100 yards. Coach parties welcome at advance notice.

LIGHT RAILWAYS

Aberystwyth – Devil's Bridge. 1 hour each way. Service: Easter and Whitsun Bank Holidays, and June – 2nd week September, twice daily. Economic party charter maximum 350. Vale of Rheidol Light Railway, British Rail, Aberystwyth.

PARKS AND GARDENS

Hidcote Manor. Groups of formal and informal gardens enclosed by hedges. Open daily, except Tue. and Fri., Easter – October, 11.00 – 20.00 or dusk. 4 miles north-east of Chipping Campden, Gloucestershire.

Spetchley Park Gardens. Fine trees and rare shrubs with red and fallow deer and ornamental water fowl. Garden centre. Teas on Sun. Open daily, April – October, 11.00 – 17.00. Sun 14.00 – 18.00. 3 miles east of Worcester, on A422.

Westonbirt Arboretum (Westonbirt 220). Shrubs chosen for autumn colourings and contrasting shapes. Rhododendrons. Refreshments April – October. Open daily all year, 10.00 – 22.00 or sundown. Near Tetbury, Gloucestershire GL8 8QS.

The Three Bays, Aberystwyth

SPAS AND HISTORIC CITIES

Gloucester. On the river Severn and once a Roman city. The magnificent cathedral dates back to Norman times. Churches: St. Mary-de-Lode; St. Nicholas; St. John the Baptist; St. Mary-de-Crypt. Places of interest: St. Oswald's Priory; Pilgrims' Arch; St. Mary's Gateway; Castle; New Inn; Regency houses in Spa Road. Parks: Hillfield Gardens; Gloucester Park; Oval Park; Lannett Park.

Worcester. The cathedral city of Worcester is the home of the world-famous Royal Worcester Porcelain. There are a number of historically interesting buildings. Churches: The Cathedral; St. Andrew's; St. Swithun's; St. Helen's. Places of interest: The Guildhall; The Greyfriars; Tudor House; Nash House; King Charles House; Queen Elizabeth's House; New Street and Friar Street; Shirehall. Museums: City Museum and Art Gallery; Tudor House Folk Museum; Elgar's Birthplace. Parks: Pitchcroft; Cheluvelt Park; Cripplegate Park; Fort Royal Park.

Hereford. The cathedral city of Hereford is situated pleasantly on the banks of the river Wye and contains many places of interest. Churches: The Cathedral; St. Peter's; All Saints. Museums: City Museum and Art Gallery; Churchill Gardens Museum; Booth Hall. Places of interest: The Old House; City Wall; Aubrey's Almshouses. Gardens and Parks: Castle Green; Redcliffe Gardens.

Cheltenham. Cheltenham is a beautiful

The Neptune Fountain, Cheltenham

spa town with a wealth of Regency houses, elegant squares, crescents and parks. Places of interest: Many fine Georgian houses; Pump Room; Parish church of St. Mary. Gardens: Promenade; Imperial Gardens; Pittville; Sandford Park and open-air swimming pool; Montpellier; Hatherley Park. Cheltenham Festival in July and Festival of Literature during October.

Aberystwyth. This coastal resort is also a University centre. The surrounding countryside is exceptionally beautiful. Castle remains, University College, National Library of Wales, Rheidol Valley Railway.

College Street, Gloucester

The Cathedral, Hereford

ZOOS

Cardiff Zoo, Weycock Road, Barry (Barry 4687). A small zoo with elephants, lions, chimpanzees fed at 16.00. Pony and donkey rides. Visitors may feed some of the animals. Also mechanical rides and amusement arcade. Light refreshments, seating 60. Open daily 10.30 – dusk. On B4266.

Birdland Zoo Gardens, Bourton-on-the-Water, Gloucestershire. 600 birds, many flying free in delightful gardens. Tropical house with outstanding collection of humming birds and penguin pool with glass side for watching underwater swimming and feeding. Open daily 10.00 – dusk. Near Northleach, off A429.

The River Severn, Worcester

Clifton & West of England Zoological Society, Clifton (Bristol 38951). Sea lions fed at 11.45 and 15.30. Lions and tigers fed at 16.00, winter at 15.00, except Sun. Licensed catering. Open 9.00 – dusk. Sun from 10.00. On A38.

41

Dudley Zoo, Worcestershire (Dudley 52401). Vultures fed 15.45, winter at 14.50, lions and tigers at 15.00, winter at 16.00. Chimpanzee tea party at 16.30. Afternoon elephant, camel and donkey rides. Visitors may feed some of the animals. Miniature railway, amusement park, trampolines and dry ski slope, castle ruins. Licensed catering seating 400. Open daily 10.00 – 18.00 or sunset, whichever is the earlier. On A4101.

Wildfowl Trust, Slimbridge, Gloucestershire (Cambridge (Glos.) 333). Over 2,500 birds of more than 160 different species. Six viewing towers and 15 hides. Visitors may feed the birds. Refreshments. Open weekdays 9.30 – dusk, Sun. from 12.00. 13 miles south-west of Gloucester, off A38. M5 exits 13 and 14.

Wildlife Park, Westbury-on-Trym, Bristol (Bristol 625112). British wildlife seen under natural conditions. Feeding bags available. Visitors can feed the seals under supervision. Refreshments, seating 100. Open daily 9.00 – dusk.

AREA FIVE

Warwickshire, Northamptonshire, Leicestershire, Huntingdonshire, Bedfordshire, Rutland, and parts of Lincolnshire.

AMUSEMENT PARKS

Wicksteed Park, Kettering, Northants. (Kettering 2475.) Miniature railway, parkland, boating lake, pet's corner, amusements, golf, bathing and paddling pool. Refreshments. Open Easter – September.

Woburn Abbey and Zoo Park. (052-525 431.) Sideshows, art gallery, craft pottery, boating pool, children's zoo, safari park, Woburn Abbey House. Open every day of the year.

The Lake, Wicksteed Park, Kettering

CASTLES

Rockingham Castle. *Commander L. M. M. Saunders Watson, RN.* Built by William the Conqueror and granted to the present family by Henry VIII. Fine pictures and furniture of all periods. Associated with Charles Dickens. Refreshments. Open Thu., Sun. and Bank Holiday Mon., Easter – September, 14.00 – 18.00. 8 miles north of Kettering, Northamptonshire, on A6003.

Warwick Castle. *The Earl of Warwick.* Fine medieval castle with towers, battlements and dungeons. Exceptional collection of armour and paintings. State rooms. Peacock gardens landscaped by "Capability" Brown. Refreshments. Open daily, March – October, 10.00 – 17.30. Warwick.

COUNTRY HOUSES

Aston Hall. *The Corporation of Birmingham.* Jacobean house with a remarkable staircase and long gallery. Magnificent plaster friezes and ceilings. Portraits and furniture of the period provided by the City Art Gallery. Refreshments. Open weekdays 10.00 – 17.00 (or dusk). Sun. from 14.00. Birmingham. 2½ miles from the city centre. (021-327 0062.)

The Castle Warwick

Burghley House. *The Marquess of Exeter.* Built by Lord Burghley, Lord High Treasurer to Elizabeth I. Lovely painted ceilings, silver fireplaces, superb collection of pictures, tapestries and furniture. Refreshments. Open daily, except Mon. and Fri., April – October, 11.00 – 17.00. Sun. from 14.00. Special times during Horse Trials. Near Stamford, Lincolnshire, off B1443. (Stamford 3302.)

Castle Ashby. *The Marquess of Northampton, D.S.O.* An Elizabethan house with original ceilings, oak panelling, staircases and an extensive collection of pictures. Refreshments. Open Sun. and Bank Holiday Mon., Easter – September, Thu. and Sat., June – August, 14.00 – 17.30. 6 miles east of Northampton, off A428.

Chacombe Priory. *Mrs. M. D. Allfrey.* A 17th century house containing a picture gallery and silver room. Refreshments. Open Sun. and Bank Holiday Mon., April – September. Sat., June – August, Fri. during August, 14.30 – 18.30. Chacombe, Oxfordshire. 2½ miles north-east of Banbury, off B4036. (Middleton Cheney 356.)

44

Chastleton House. *Alan Clutton-Brock, Esq.* A 17th century house with fine plasterwork, panelling and furniture. Refreshments. Open daily, except Wed., 10.30 – 13.00 and 14.00 – 17.30. Sun., 14.00 – 16.00. 5 miles north west of Chipping Norton, Oxfordshire. (Barton-on-the-Heath 355.)

Compton Wynyates. *The Marquess of Northampton, D.S.O.* Built in 1480 and largely fortified in 1520. The battlemented walls and twisted chimneys, together with the interior, have remained virtually unaltered. Associations with Henry VIII. Open Wed., Sat. and Bank Holidays from April – September. Sun., June – August, 14.00 – 17.30. 10 miles west of Banbury, Warwickshire, off B4035.

Stapleford
Lion Reserve

Woburn Abbey and Zoo. *The Duke of Bedford.* An 18th century mansion set in magnificent parkland which includes a wild animal kingdom. The house contains collections of china, books, pictures, silver, historical documents, modern art gallery, crafts centre and antique market. The grounds include a pets' corner and a children's playground. Refreshments and picnic tables. Open daily 11.30 – 18.00. Sun. until 9.00. Mid-September to October until 19.30. Sun. until 18.30. Woburn, A50 and off M1 (Junctions 12 or 13). (Woburn 666.)

Ragley Hall. *The Marquess of Hertford.* A 17th century house with some exceptional pictures, china and furniture. Cricket in the park. Refreshments. Open Tue., Wed., Thu., Sat. and Sun., Bank Holiday Mon., Easter – September, 14.00 – 17.30. Bank Holidays from 12.00. 2 miles south-west of Alcester, Warwickshire, on A435.

Stanford Hall. *Lord and Lady Braye.* A William and Mary house, dating from

1690. The house contains an antique kitchen with period utensils, furniture, family pictures and costumes. Museum of vintage cars and motor cycles. Walled rose garden, old forge, pottery, nature trail. Refreshments. Open Thu., Sat. and Sun., Easter – September, 14.30 – 18.00. Bank Holidays from 12.00. Swinford, Leicestershire, 7½ miles northeast of Rugby, off B5414. (Swinford 250.)

Stapleford Park House. *Lord and Lady Gretton.* A restored 17th century house containing pictures, tapestries and furniture. Park with a miniature railway and a Lion reserve. Refreshments. Open Thu., Sun. and Bank Holiday Mon., May – September, 14.30 – 18.30. 5 miles east of Melton Mowbray, Leicestershire, off B676.

FACTORY TOURS AND CRAFT SHOPS

Ceramic Ornaments, also hand etched and printed colour etchings. Open any reasonable time by appointment. John & Heather Brunsdon, 17 Bedford Street, Woburn, Bedfordshire. (Woburn 606.)

Cosmetics. Trip lasts 2 hours. No children under 12. Visits: Mon. – Fri., 10.00 and 14.00. Parties must give 12 months' notice. Maximum party number 20. Contact: Avon Cosmetics Ltd., Nunn's Mills Road, Northampton. Northampton (34722, ex 227.)

Jewellery. Individual gold and silver jewellery and semi-precious stones mounted in a wide range of goods. Open: Daily 10.00 – 17.00. Rings & Things, High Street, Buckden, Huntingdonshire. (Buckden 836.)

Knitwear. Made on hand machines with wide range of patterns. Open any reasonable time by appointment. Patrice Knitwear, 57-9 High Street, Sharnbrook, Bedfordshire.

Laundry. Trip lasts 1½ hours. Visits: Mon. – Fri., 14.30. Parties must give 1 weeks' notice. Maximum party number 20. Contact: The Co-operative Society Ltd., Holyhead Road, Birmingham 21.

Motor Cars. Trip lasts 2 hours. No children under 14. Visits: Mon. – Fri., 10.15 – 13.45. Parties must give 3 months' notice. Maximum party number 30. Contact: Vauxhall Motors Ltd., Luton. (Luton 21122, ex 3321.)

Motor Cars. Trip lasts 2¼ hours. Visits: Mon. – Thu., 14.15. Parties must give 3 months' notice. Maximum party number 20. Contact: Public Relations Department, Rover Co. Ltd., Lode Lane, Solihull, Warwickshire. (021-743 4242.)

Paintings. Fine art and botanical

paintings of flowers, fruits, butterflies, and flower miniatures. Open: Any reasonable time by appointment. Dorothy Bovey, Killock Ho, Laughton, Husbands Bosworth, near Rugby, Leicestershire. Fleckney 278.

Pictures, original screen prints, paintings and local craftwork. Open: Tue. – Sun. 9.00 – 17.00. The Print Workshop, 91 High Street, Somersham, Huntingdonshire. (Somersham 636.)

Painting Repairs. Cleaning and restoring oil paintings. Open any reasonable time by appointment. C. B. Savage, 64 Booth Lane South, Weston Favell. (Northampton 41948.)

Pottery. Stoneware tableware, lamp bases, wall plaques, animal sculptures, especially owls and bulls, named mugs for children. Open any reasonable time by appointment. Marion Aldis, Zion House Pottery, South Croxton, Leicester LE7 8RL. (Gaddesby 363.)

Pottery. Slipware casseroles and oven pots, tea and coffee sets, mugs, bowls, etc. Open daily 8.30 – 18.00, Sat and Sun. 9.30 – 12.30. Appointment advisable. Elizabeth Blundell, Pumphouse Pottery, Avon Dassett, near Leamington Spa. (Farnborough, Warwicks. 317.)

Rocking Chairs. Spindle and ladderback rocking chairs, also dining chairs and stools. Open: 8.00 – 18.00 or any reasonable time by appointment. Neville Neal, Stockton, near Rugby, Warwickshire.

Railway Stock. No parties. Advance notice essential as visits are limited. Visits: Mon. – Thu., 14.30 – 16.15. Contact: Metropolitan-Cammell Ltd., PO Box 248, Leigh Road, Birmingham B8 2YJ. (021-327 4777.)

Saddlery and Harness and other leatherwork. Also belts and sheepskin rugs. Open daily, except Sun., 9.00 – 18.00. Osier Handcrafts, The Old Mill, Gravenhurst, Bedfordshire. (Shillington 269.)

Wrought Ironwork. Fire baskets, screens, candlesticks, weather vanes, light brackets. Open weekdays 8.00 – 17.00, Sat. till 12.00. Pury End Forge, Carey's Road, Paulerspury, Northamptonshire.

Shuttleworth Collection

INNS AND COACHING HOUSES

The Angel (A6, 427 and 508), High Street, Market Harborough, Leicestershire (Market Harborough 3123). Built in the 16th century, and situated midway between London and Manchester, it was long one of the most flourishing coaching houses. Today there is a lovely period dining room and a good choice of 12 main courses. Parking on premises. Coach parties of up to 48, by appointment.

The Three Swans, High Street, Market Harborough, Leicestershire (Market Harborough 3247). Built towards the

end of the 14th century, it was originally a single swan or, to be more precise, "Ye Sygne of Swanns" and acquired the three necks and a fine wrought iron sign in the 17th century. It was once owned and managed by J. Fothergill who wrote *An Innkeeper's Diary*. Specialities: Carpet bag steak, beef Stroganoff, clam steak, scallops St. Jacques. Free house. Coach parties of up to 60, by appointment.

The White Swan (A34, 46, 422 and 439), Rother Street, Stratford-upon-Avon, Warwickshire (Stratford 3606). The inn dates from before Shakespeare, who must have known it well as a child, for he lived two minutes away. It has hardly altered so he must also have known the remarkable mural of the story of Tobit which is in the lounge. Free house. Parking in Market Square. Coach parties up to 120 welcome, by appointment.

MUSEUMS

Museum of Science & Industry. Exhibits of locomotives, steam and internal combustion engines, small arms, mechanical musical instruments, machine tools, scientific apparatus, aircraft and aircraft engines. Open daily 10.00 – 17.00. Sat. until 17.30. Sun. 14.00 – 17.30. Newhall Street, Birmingham.

The Shuttleworth Collection. *The Richard Ormonde Shuttleworth Remembrance Trust.* An historic collection of aircraft and flying machines. The museum also contains cars, carriages and bicycles. Open daily 10.00 – 17.00. Old Warden, Bedfordshire, 2 miles west of Biggleswade, off A1.

GARDENS

Wrest Park (01-834 9040, ex 325). Examples of methods of landscape gardening between 18th and 19th century. Open Sat., Sun and Bank Holiday Mon. April – September, 10.00 – 19.00. April to 17.30. Silsoe, 10 miles north of Luton. Refreshments.

PLEASURE FLIGHTS

Luton Airport. Luton Flying Club (Luton 24426). Flights daily. Licensed restaurant.

HISTORIC TOWNS

Stratford-upon-Avon. The birthplace of William Shakespeare with its many picturesque buildings which provide interesting links with the bard. Churches: Holy Trinity; Guild Chapel. Buildings

47

of interest: Royal Shakespeare Theatre; Church Street Almshouses; Shakespeare's Birthplace; Grammar School; Anne Hathaway's Cottage; Harvard House; New Place; Garrick Inn; Clopton Bridge. Parks: New Place Gardens. River trips from Bancroft Gardens and Swan's Nest Boathouse.

ZOOS

Coventry Zoo Park, Whitley Common (Coventry 301772). Designed to provide good viewing of animals in both wet and dry weather. Domed dolphinarium, children's corner. Visitors may feed the animals. Licensed restaurant. Open daily 10.00 – dusk. Off A45.

Peakirk Waterfowl Gardens, Northants (Glinton 271). Over 100 species of ducks, geese and swans as well as flamingos and other exotic waterfowl. Visitors may feed the birds. Refreshments. Open daily 9.30 – 17.30, winter to 16.30. Sun. from 12.00. Peakirk, 7 miles north of Peterborough, off A15.

Southam Zoo Farm, Daventry Road, Southam, Leamington Spa, Warwickshire (Southam 2431). A small private zoo with lions, leopards, pumas, bears, birds of prey. Pets' corner. Visitors may feed some of the animals. Free swings and swing boats. Refreshments seating 30. Open daily Easter – October, 10.00 dusk. ½ mile from Southam, on A425.

Stagsden Bird Gardens, Stagsden, Bedfordshire (Oakley 2745). Collection of rare pheasants and waterfowl, parakeets and other exotic birds as well as old breeds of poultry and bantams. Refreshments. Open daily 11.00 – dusk or 19.00, whichever is earlier. 2 miles from Bedford, off A422.

Twycross Zoo, near Atherstone, Leicestershire (Twycross 250). Fine private collection, modern reptile house, aviary. Chimps' teaparty, elephants' bathtime. Sealions and penguins. Pets' corner. Donkey and miniature train rides. Refreshments, seating 700. Open daily 10.00 – 18.00, winter till dusk. 11 miles north of Nuneaton on A444.

Whipsnade Park, Dunstable, Bedfordshire LU6 2LF (Whipsnade 471). 2,000 animals and birds in maximum freedom in enclosures and paddocks covering 500 acres. Rhino park with steam railway. Children's zoo corner. Feeding times (winter months ½ hour earlier): sealions 14.30, Polar bears 15.00, Kodiak bears 15.15, lions 15.30, tigers 15.45, penguins 16.15. Metalled roads and road train. Telescopes and invalid chairs for hire. Refreshments. Open daily 10.00 – 19.00. B4540, off M1.

AREA SIX

Norfolk, Suffolk, Cambridgeshire, Essex, Hertfordshire.

BOAT EXCURSIONS

Fritton Lake, near Great Yarmouth, Norfolk. Two mile long lake with fishing, boating, gardens, children's playground. Tea room and picnic areas. Open daily Easter – October.

The River Thurne and Thurne Mill, Norfolk Broads

Tuesday and Thursday 10.00 June – September. Great Yarmouth 7½ hours Horning return.

Bure. Broads Tours Ltd., Wroxham, Norwich NOR 06Z. (Wroxham 2207.) Season Easter – September. Private party charter, minimum 30, maximum 600. Teas. Wroxham return 1 hour. Wroxham 2 hours Ranworth, leaving 11.00, 13.00 and 15.15. Wroxham half-day South Walsham Broads, leaving 15.00. Wroxham day trip, Salhouse, Tuesday and Friday, 11.00.

Waveney. Pleasure Steamers Ltd., Riverside, Southtown, Great Yarmouth. (Great Yarmouth 2366.) Licensed, refreshments. Wednesday, 10.30 June – September. Great Yarmouth 6½ hours, St. Olaves. Great Yarmouth 2 hours, Broadlands.

Yare. Pleasure Steamers Ltd., 1 Riverside, Southtown, Great Yarmouth. (Great Yarmouth 2366.) Licensed, refreshments. Services June – September. Great Yarmouth 2 hours, Breydon Water, Sun., Mon., Tue., Thur. & Fri. 10.30 and 14.45. Great Yarmouth 3½ hours, Reedham. Wed. & Sun. 14.45. Great Yarmouth 7 hours, Oulton Broad. Mon. & Fri. 10.30.

River Waveney at Beccles

Bure. Pleasure Steamers Ltd., 1 Riverside, Southtown, Great Yarmouth. (Great Yarmouth 2366.) Licensed, refreshments.

CASTLES

Caister Castle. *P. R. Hill, Esq.* Ruins of a 15th century moated castle with a 100-foot tower. Collection of early motor cars. Refreshments. Open mid-May to October, Mon. – Sat. 10.30 – 17.30. Sun. during October, afternoons. 3 miles north of Great Yarmouth, Norfolk, off A1064.

Hedingham Castle. *Miss Majendie and Dr. Blackie.* Large Norman keep and Tudor bridge. Open Tue., Thur., Sat. and Bank Holiday Mon., May – September, 14.00 – 18.00. Castle Hedingham, Essex, on B1058.

COUNTRY HOUSES

Hatfield House. *The Marquess of Salisbury.* Tudor palace, childhood home of Elizabeth I. Jacobean house is the ancestral home of the Cecil family and contains portraits, furniture and relics of Queen Elizabeth I. Refreshments. Garden. Open daily, except Mon., April – September and Bank Holiday, 12.00 – 17.00. Sun. 14.00 – 17.30. Hatfield, Hertfordshire. (Hatfield 62823.)

Holkham Hall. *The Earl of Leicester, M.V.O., D.L.* An 18th century Palladian house with marble hall and State rooms containing an extensive collection of pictures, tapestries, statuary and furnishings. Refreshments. Open Thu., June – September. Mon., July – August and Bank Holidays, 14.00 – 17.00. 2 miles west of Wells, Norfolk, on A149.

Ickworth. *The National Trust.* An 18th century circular architectural curiosity with a collection of pictures, furniture and silver. Teas. Open Wed., Thu., Sat.,

Sun. and Bank Holiday Mon. from April – September, 14.00 – 18.00. 3 miles south-west of Bury St. Edmunds, Suffolk, off A143.

Knebworth House. *Lord and Lady Cobbold.* A Gothicised Tudor mansion with an exceptional banqueting hall. Former home of Bulwer-Lytton and associated with Dickens. Collection of

50

Elizabethan portraits and 17th and 18th century furniture, paintings, books and documents. Formal gardens and country park. Refreshments. Miniature railway and children's amusements. Open Tue. – Fri., April – September. Sat. and Sun., June – September, 14.00 – 17.00. Old Knebworth, Hertfordshire, 1 mile from Stevenage, A1(M). (Knebworth 2661.)

Layer Marney Tower. *Major and Mrs. Gerald Charrington.* An unfinished Tudor brick mansion built in 1520 with a unique eight-storied tower gate house. Open Sun., Tue., Thu. and Bank Holiday April – October, 14.00 – 18.00. Near Tiptree, Essex, off B1022. (Birch 202.)

Somerleyton Hall. *Lord and Lady Somerleyton.* 16th century buildings with 19th century additions. Carvings, tapestries and pictures. Garden with maze, nature trail and miniature railway. Teas. Open Sun., Thu. and Bank Holiday Mon., Easter – October. Tue., July and August, 14.00 – 18.00. 5 miles northwest of Lowestoft, off B1074.

FACTORY TOURS AND CRAFT SHOPS

Camera Films. Colour processing. No children under 14. Visits: Mon. – Thu., November – July, individuals at 10.00, parties at 14.00. April – July, parties at 18.00. Parties must give 2 months' notice. Maximum number 20. Kodak Ltd., Maylands Avenue, Hemel Hempstead, Hertfordshire.

Cameras. Manufacture of cameras and apparatus, microfilmers and complex processing machines. No children under 14. Visits: Mon. – Fri., 14.00. Parties must give 2 months' notice. Maximum party number 20. Kodak Ltd., Gunnells Wood Road, Stevenage, Hertfordshire.

Glass Engraving by diamond point. Open any reasonable time, by appointment. Felix White, The Flints, Great Barton, Bury St. Edmunds, Suffolk. (Gt. Barton 675).

Ironwork. Hand-forged wrought ironwork including grates, balustrades, staircases and firedogs. Open: Mon. – Fri. 8.00 – 17.00 by appointment. The Elstree Forge, 21 High Street, Elstree, Borehamwood, Hertfordshire. (01-953 2553.)

Jigsaw Puzzles. Children's puzzles, educational and religious pastimes. Open daily 9.00 – 19.00. W. R. Kelly, Mill Green, Stonham Aspal, Stowmarket, Suffolk. (Stonham 263).

Motor Cars. Trip lasts 2¼ hours. No children under 10. Visits: Mon. – Fri., 9.45 and 13.30. Parties must give 3 months' notice. Maximum party number 40. Contact: The Ford Motor Co. Ltd., Dagenham, Essex. (01-592 4591 ex 239.)

Pottery. Domestic stoneware and individual pieces. Open daily 9.00 – 20.00. Abington Pottery, 26 High Street, Little Abington. (Cambridge 891-723.)

Rushwork. Table mats, log baskets, carpets, chairs, shopping baskets, osier baskets and chairs. Open: Mon. – Fri. 9.00 – 17.00. Deben Rush Weavers, High Street, Debenham, Stowmarket, Suffolk. (Debenham 349).

Stained Glass. Windows, panels, sculptural ceramics. Open any reasonable time by appointment. St. Crispin's Glass, 28 St. Albans Road, Codicote, near Welwyn, Herts. (Codicote 335.)

Stoneware. Wide range of domestic stoneware, mugs, plates, jugs, bowls and large individual pieces. Open any reasonable time by appointment. Needham Pottery, Wood Farm, Linstead Magna, Halesworth, Suffolk. (Linstead 301).

Kodak colour film

Tiles. Multi-coloured in unusual glazes and large tile pictures. Open: Mon. – Fri. 9.30 – 17.30., Sat. till 13.00. Intaglio Designs, 5 White Hart Street, Thetford, Norfolk. (Thetford 2708.)

Wooden Toys. Trains, carts, doll cradles, animals, vehicles, etc., for children of all ages. Open: Mon. – Sat. 9.00 – 17.30. Twintoys, Molls Yard, Thurton, Norwich. (Thurton 245.)

INNS AND COACHING HOUSES

Lion Hotel (A12, 133, 134 and 604), High Street, Colchester, Essex (Colchester 77986). A 16th century inn with black and white front, a wealth of oak beams and fine wood carving. Specialities: Steak and schnitzel. Free house. Coach parties up to 40 welcome by appointment.

The Fighting Cocks (A5, 6 and 414). Abbey Mill Lane, St. Albans (St. Albans 65830). Claimed to be the oldest licensed inhabited house in England, dating from AD 795. It is on the site of part of the St. Alban's Abbey. Cold meat platters and hot jacket potatoes. Coach parties of up to 75 welcome.

The Magpie (A45 and 140), Norwich Road, Stonham Parva, Stowmarket, Suffolk (Stonham 287). In 1481 the place was owned by the local parson and it eventually became the property of the parish. When it was bought by a brewery the money went towards paying for the village water system. The inn is remarkable for having a gallows sign reaching right across the road. Music Saturday and Sunday evening. Affiliated transport cafe next door, open 7.45 – 16.00. Coach parties up to 60 welcome.

The Sun (A12), Dedham, Essex (Dedham 3351). Built in 1490, quite a lot of the original building remains intact, including the outside staircase in the yard. Specialities: Game in season, fresh fish and typical English fare. Coach parties welcome by appointment.

MUSEUMS

Rhodes Memorial Museum and Commonwealth Centre. An early 19th century house containing relics and illustrations showing the life and work of Cecil Rhodes and the history of Southern and Central Africa. Open daily 10.00 – 16.00. Sun. by appointment only. South Road, Bishop's Stortford, Hertfordshire.

Shaw's Corner. *The National Trust.* The house that George Bernard Shaw occupied from 1906 until his death in

Ye Old Fighting Cocks, St. Albans

1950. Open daily, except Tue, mid-January – December, 11.00 – 13.00 and 14.00 – 18.00 (or dusk). Ayot St. Lawrence, Hertfordshire, 3 miles west of Welwyn, off A1.

Verulamium Museum. Situated on the site of the Roman city of Verulamium. Large collection of Roman remains including three fine mosaic floors and theatre. Open daily 10.00 – 17.30. Sun. from 14.00. Winter weekdays until 16.00. St. Michael's, St. Albans, Hertfordshire.

Zoological Museum. Specimens of animals from throughout the world. Open daily 10.00 – 17.00. Sun. from 14.00. Akeman Street, Tring, Hertfordshire.

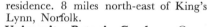

Roman Theatre, Verulamium, St. Albans

St. John's College from Trinity Bridge, Cambridge

GARDENS

Sandringham. Refreshments. Open Tue., Wed., Thu. and Bank Holiday Mon., April – September. Fri., June – August, 11.00 – 17.00. Closed when a member of the Royal Family is in residence. 8 miles north-east of King's Lynn, Norfolk.

University Botanic Gardens. Open daily, except Sun., all year, 8.00 – 20.00 or dusk. Cambridge.

PLEASURE FLIGHTS

North Denes Aerodrome. Anglian Air Charter Ltd., Great Yarmouth. (Gt. Yarmouth 4426). Flights from mid-May – October, other months by appointment. Refreshments.

Stansted Airport. Skywork Ltd. (Bishops Stortford 502380).

Stapleford Aerodrome. Thurston Aviation Ltd., near Hertford (Stapleford 341). Flights, including night flights, all year. Licensed restaurant.

HISTORIC TOWNS

Cambridge. One of the most beautiful towns in Britain, Cambridge is justly proud of its position and heritage. There are many interesting places to see, particularly the Colleges and other University buildings. There are excellent shopping facilities and the city is renowned for its many fine bookshops.

53

Elm Hill, Norwich

Colchester. Colchester was formerly a Bronze Age settlement and later, a Roman fortress. The town boasts many fine buildings ranging from the 15th century to the present day and is still surrounded by Roman walls. Churches: Holy Trinity; St. Peter's; St. James; St. Botolph's. Museums: The Castle; Minores Art Gallery. Historical buildings: Holly Trees; Old Siege House; Bourn Mill; St. John's Abbey Gateway; Balkern Gate.

Norwich. The splendidly impressive cathedral city of Norwich with its many churches, castle and excellent shopping facilities has plenty to attract the visitor. Churches: The Cathedral; St. Andrew; St. Gregory; St. Helen; St. Mary-at-Coslany; St. Micheal-at-Coslany; St. Michael-at-Plea; St. Peter Hungate; St. Peter Mancroft; St. Stephen. Museums: Castle Museum; Strangers' Hall; Bridewell Museum; St. Andrew's Hall; St. Peter Hungate Church. Places of interest: Assembly House; The Music House; Maddermarket; The Guildhall; Pull's Ferry; City Hall. Parks: Chapel Field Gardens; Earlham Park; Eaton Park; Mousehold Heath; Waterloo Park; Wensum Park; Woodrow Pilling Park.

St. Albans. Those who are interested in Roman archaeology will find the site of Verulamium well worth visiting in addi-

Lily Pond and Castle, Colchester

Churches: St. Benet's; St. Mary-the-Great; St. Andrew-the-Less; St. Botolph's; St. Edward's; St. Mary-the-Less; St. Mary Magdalene; St. Michael's; St. Sepulchre. Museums: Fitzwilliam Museum; Scott Polar Research Institute; Folk Gallery; Whipple Museum of the History of Science; Arts Council Gallery. Historical buildings: College buildings and chapels, notably King's College Chapel, Senate House, Barnwell Abbey House, Eagle Inn, Old Library. Gardens: Botanic Gardens; College gardens; The Backs; Midsummer Common; Jesus Green. River trips: Punts for hire at Mill Bridge or Anchor Inn.

tion to the city's 12th – 13th century Abbey. Churches: Abbey; St. Michael's; St. Stephen's. Museum: Verulamium. Places of interest: The Clock Tower; Monastery Gateway; The Fighting Cocks; White Hart Hotel; Bleak House; French Row.

THE SEASIDE

Clacton-on-Sea. Attractions: Band, model village, crazy golf, amusement pier, the Sussex amusement park, two cinemas, two theatres, bingo, putting. Launch trips by Eagle Steamers Ltd. from the pierhead and boat trips from the beach east and west of the pier.

Dolphinarium. Flights from the Air Strip, West Road. Live shows: Concerts at the Princes Theatre, revue at the Westcliff Pavilion and Ocean Theatres. Dancing: Westcliff Hotel, Marine Parade West and the Town Hall ballroom. Children's amusements: Sand, kiddies' playground, Punch & Judy, donkey and pony rides, zoo, model yacht pond, miniature railway. Item of interest: Lifeboat house.

Great Yarmouth & Gorleston. Seaside attractions: Britannia and Wellington pleasure piers, Pleasure Beach, Joyland amusement parks, model village, waxworks, aqua-zoo, Venetian waterways, boating lakes, two swimming pools (one heated), bowls, tennis, putting, golf, croquet, ten-pin bowling, sea and river trips, greyhound racing, stock car racing, pleasure flights by Air Anglia Ltd, Illuminations, May – September, four cinemas. Children's amusements: Beach, Punch & Judy, yacht pond and paddling pool, pony rides, kiddies' cars, crazy golf, trampolines, roller skating. Live shows: Variety, ABC Theatre, Britannia Theatre, Wellington Pavilion. Music Hall, Gorleston Pavilion; Comedy play, Windmill Theatre; Band and artistes, Tyrolean Biergarten; Circus, The Hippodrome. Dancing: Tiffany's. Band shows, competitions and wrestling: Marina open-air theatre. Places of interest: 11th century Parish Church; 13th century Tollhouse; old merchant's house; old town walls and towers; East Anglian Maritime Museum; the port; open-air market (Wed. and Sat.).

Hunstanton. Seaside attractions: Amusement pier, South Beach and Beach Terrace, amusement parks, band. Launch trips, cinema, crazy golf, croquet, roller skating, water ski-ing. Children's amusements: Beach, donkey and pony rides, boating and paddling

pools. Live shows: Dancing: Kit Kat, Casino and Pier Ballrooms. Places of interest: Hunstanton Hall; Seal Island.

Lowestoft. Seaside attractions: Two amusement piers, band. Illuminations throughout the season, two cinemas, two theatres, bowls, tennis, trampolines, bingo. Children's amusements: Sand, kiddies' corner, miniature railway, Punch & Judy, boating pools. Live shows: Concert party: Sparrow's Nest. Dancing: Pier Pavilion and South Pier. Places of interest: South Pier high level observation tower; Lighthouse at Yarmouth Road; Fish Market; Oulton Broad.

Southend-on-Sea. Seaside attractions: Band, five cinemas, two theatres, model railway, Dolphinarium, passing shipping, aquarium, amusement pier, Kursaal amusement park, Ten-pin bowling. Illuminations, mid-August – October. Children's amusements: Clean sands, Peter Pan's Playground, Punch & Judy, boating and paddling pool, miniature railway. Live shows: Summer show: Pier Head. Dancing: Kursaal Ballroom and various hotels. Items of interest: Prittlewell Priory and Museum; Lifeboat slipway; South-east Essex Museum; Beecroft Art Gallery.

Walton-on-the-Naze and Frinton-on-Sea. Seaside attractions: Amusement pier, launch trips from Albion Breakwater, fairground, bingo, tennis, bowls, pleasure flights from Clacton Air Strip. Illuminations throughout the season.

Children's Amusements: Sand, Punch & Judy, pony rides, boating pool. Live shows: Straight plays: Frinton Summer Theatre. Dancing: Pier Hotel (Sat. only), Martello Camp and Round Gardens Restaurant. Places of interest: Walton Backwaters; 18th century Navigation Tower.

ZOOS

Banham Zoo, Banham, Norfolk NOR 05X (Quidenham 383). Fifteen acres with a breeding colony of woolly monkeys, otters, dingoes, sealions, wolves and tropical and strange birds. Monkeys fed in summer from 15.00. Refreshments, seating 30. Open daily 10.30 – 18.30. Off A11.

Colchester Zoo, Stanway Hall, Essex (Birch 253). General zoo covering 40 acres, with African Game reserve. Also model railway, amusement arcade and exhibition hall. Visitors may feed the animals. Light refreshments. Open weekdays 9.30 – dusk, Sun. 10.00 – 18.00. West of Colchester on B1022.

Kelling Park Aviaries, Weybourne Road, Holt, Norfolk (Holt 2235). Tropical birds including ostriches, cassowaries, storks, flamingos, lories and cockatoos. Refreshments, seating 90. Open daily April – October, 10.30 – 18.30.

Mole Hall Wildlife Park, Widdington, Newport, Essex (Newport 400). Woolly monkey colony, chimpanzees and other mammals and also birds. Visitors may feed some of the animals. Set in the grounds of an old moated house. Otters fed 15.30. Light refreshments. Open daily 10.30 – 18.00. Off A11.

Nature Park, Cromer, Norfolk (Cromer 2216). Ten acres of lawns and gardens with pools and aviaries with 150 exotic birds and, in winter, north European migrants. Donkey rides Sun. at 15.00. Visitors may feed the animals. Refreshments, seating 100. Open daily 10.00 – 18.00.

Petsenta, Norton, Bury St. Edmunds, Suffolk (Pakenham 340). A combination of birds, animals and flowers set in four acres of gardens. Refreshments. Open daily 10.00 – dusk. On A1088.

Wildlife Park, Great Witchingham, Norwich 65X (Great Witchingham 274). British and European mammals and birds, especially pheasants, in large enclosures set in 30 acres of parkland. Licensed restaurant. Open daily 10.30 – 18.30 or sunset whichever is earlier. 12 miles from Norwich, on A1067.

AREA SEVEN

Buckinghamshire, Berkshire, Oxfordshire, Surrey, London, Kent, Middlesex, Sussex, Hampshire.

AMUSEMENT PARKS

Chessington Park and Zoo, Chessington, Surrey. (Epsom 27227.) Fairground amusements, circus on summer afternoons, model village. Licensed restaurants, cafeterias, marquees for parties. Open 9.30 – 20.00 (or dusk). Winter 10.00 – 16.00.

Battersea Pleasure Gardens, London S.W.11. (01-228 2226.) Funfair, rides, games, sideshows, performing dolphins, children's zoo. Licensed catering seating 750. Open daily Easter – September, 14.00 – 22.00.

BOAT EXCURSIONS

Regent's Canal, London. Jason's Trips, Canaletto Gallery, 60 Blomfield Road, W.9. (01-286 3428.) Economic charter, maximum 60. Several services daily, Whitsun – September, otherwise weekends only. Paddington 1 hour 20 mins; Camden Town, Paddington, Greenford, leaving 18.00 daily mid-July and August only. Paddington, Harlesden 19.00 daily mid-July and August only.

Thames. Salter Bros. Ltd., Kingston-upon-Thames. (Kingston 7313.) Economic party charter, minimum 100, maximum 200. Morning and afternoon service 1st week May – 2nd week September. Windsor 65 mins; Runnymede 20 mins; Staines 45 mins; Chertsey. Chertsey 50 mins; Walton-on-Thames. Walton-on-Thames ¾ hour; Hampton Court ½ hour; Kingston.

Thames. Salter Bros. Ltd., Folly Bridge, Oxford. (Oxford 43421.) Morning and afternoon services. 1st week May – 2nd week September. Party charter, minimum 100, maximum 200. Wallingford 1¼ hours; Goring Lock ¾ hour; Pangbourne 1 hour. Reading: Reading 2 hours; Henley 1¾ hours; Marlow 1¼ hours; Maidenhead 1½ hours; Windsor 1 hour; Runnymede 20 mins; Staines 45 mins; Chertsey.

Thames. Salter Bros. Ltd., Folly Bridge, Oxford. (Oxford 43421.) Economic party charter, minimum 100, maximum 200. Service two or more times daily, 1st week May – 2nd week September. Oxford 1½ hours, Abingdon.

The Lock Bridge, Richmond

58

The Castle, Bodiam

Thames. Arthur Jacobs Ltd., Thames Hotel, Windsor. (Windsor 62933.) Economic party charter, minimum 50, maximum 200.

CASTLES

Chiddingstone Castle. *Denys E. Bower, Esq.* An 18th century Gothic revival encasing old manor house. Royal Stuart and Jacobite portraits and relics. Ancient Egyptian, Japanese and Buddhist antiques. Open daily except Mon., Easter – October, 14.00 – 17.30. Sun. and Bank Holiday Mon. from 11.30. Chiddingstone, Kent, 5 miles east of Edenbridge.

Hever Castle. *Lord and Lady Astor.* Dates from 13th – 15th centuries. Former home of Anne Boleyn. Formal Italian gardens, topiary, classical statuary. Refreshments. Open Wed., Sun. and Bank Holiday Mon., Easter to mid-October, 13.00 – 19.00. 3 miles south-east of Edenbridge, Kent, off B2026.

Lympne Castle. *H. Margary, Esq.* Rebuilt about 1360. Magnificent views over Romney marshes. Refreshments. Open Wed., Sun. and Bank Holiday Mon., April – October. Daily July – September, 10.30 – 13.00 and 14.30 – 18.00. 3 miles north-west of Hythe, Kent, off B2067.

Powderham Castle. *The Earl of Devon.* Built during the 14th century but altered in the 18th and 19th centuries. Stuart and Regency furniture and portraits. Parkland with deer. Falconry on Tuesdays. Cream teas. Open Sun., Tue., Wed. and Thu., June — August. Mon. and Fri., mid-July and August, 14.00 – 18.00. Kenton, Devon. 8 miles south-west of Exeter, A379.

Bodiam Castle. *The National Trust.* Well preserved ruins of 14th century moated curtain wall castle. Open weekdays 10.00 – 19.00 (or dusk). Sun., April – September, 10.00 – 19.00. 3 miles south of Hawkhurst, Sussex, on A229.

Broughton Castle. *Lord and Lady Saye and Sele.* Originally built in 1300 and enlarged in 1554 with a gatehouse and moat. Associations with the Civil War. Open Wed. and Bank Holiday Mon., April – September. 1st and 2nd Sun. in month from June – September, 14.00 – 17.00. 2½ miles south-west of Banbury, Oxfordshire.

59

Windsor Castle. A royal home for nearly a thousand years. Medieval precincts, state apartments with pictures, furniture and porcelain. St. George's Chapel. Precincts open daily from 10.00 until sunset. State apartments open on weekdays between 11.00 – 17.00, and until 15.00 from November – February. March, April and October until 16.00. Sun. 13.30 – 17.00, November – April until 16.00. St. George's Chapel open daily from 11.00 – 15.45, Fri. from 13.00 and Sun. from 14.30.

CAVES

Hell Fire Caves, High Wycombe, Buckinghamshire. (High Wycombe 24411.) Created for orgies by the Regency bucks. Trip lasts $\frac{1}{2}$ hour. Nearby attractions in summer include West Wycombe Park, the Dashwood family mausoleum, the golden ball, model world and donkey stud. Open Sun. and daily March – September, 14.00 – 19.00. Weekdays mid-July to September from 11.00.

The Norman Gate, Windsor

Palace House, Beaulieu

COUNTRY HOUSES.

Bateman's. *The National Trust.* The 17th century house where Rudyard Kipling once lived. Gardens and a riverside walk. Teas. Open daily, except Fri., March – October, 11.00 – 12.30 and 14.00 – 18.00. Sat. and Sun. from 14.00. Bank Holiday Mon. from 11.00. 2 miles south of Burwash, Sussex. A265. (Burwash 302.)
Beaulieu Palace House. *Lord Montagu of Beaulieu.* Ancestral home and formerly the Great Gatehouse of Beaulieu Abbey. Gardens and abbey ruins. National Motor Museum. Refreshments. Open daily, 10.00 – 18.00. November – March, until 17.00. 5 miles from Lymington, Hampshire. (Beaulieu 374.)

Blenheim Palace. *The Duke of Marlborough.* One of Sir John Vanbrugh's finest buildings, the palace houses a collection of china, paintings, tapestries and furniture. The grounds were landscaped by "Capability" Brown. The house was the birthplace of Sir Winston Churchill in 1874. Refreshments. Open daily, except Fri., April – October, 13.00 – 18.00. South-west of Woodstock, Oxfordshire, off A34. (0993-811325.)

Breamore House. *Sir Westrow Hulse, Bart.* Elizabethan manor house with fine paintings, tapestries and furniture. Countryside and carriage museums. Teas. Open daily, except Mon. and Fri., Easter – September, 14.00 – 18.00. Breamore, Hampshire, 8 miles south of Salisbury, A338. (Breamore 233.)

Claydon House. *The Verney family.* An 18th century house with rococo decorated State rooms. Teas. Open daily, except Mon. and Tue. after Bank Holidays. March – October, 14.00 – 18.00. 3½ miles south-west of Winslow, Buckinghamshire, off A413. (Steeple Claydon 349.)

Firle Place. *Viscount Gage, K.C.V.O.* Tudor home belonging to the Gage family since the 15th century although it was altered considerably in 1730. Fine collection of pictures, furniture and Sèvres china. Teas. Open Wed. and Thu., June – September, 14.15 – 17.30. Sun. and Bank Holiday Mon., 15.00 – 18.00. 5 miles south-east of Lewes, Sussex, on A27.

Glynde Place. *Mrs. Humphrey Brand.* A 16th century flint and brick house with fine collection of pictures, Soldani bronzes and needlework. Teas. Open Thu., Sat., Sun. and Bank Holiday Mon., May – September, 14.15 – 17.30. 4 miles south-east of Lewes, Sussex, off A27. (Glynde 229.)

Great Dixter. *Mrs. Nathaniel Lloyd.* A 15th century half-timbered house with gardens designed by Lutyens. Open daily, except Mon. and Bank Holidays, mid-May – September, 14.00 – 17.00. Northiam, 8 miles north-west of Rye, Sussex. (Northiam 3160.)

Hampton Court. The palace built for Cardinal Wolsey and later presented to the sovereign. The building has many royal associations and contains State rooms, tapestries and pictures. Superb gardens. Open daily 9.30 – 18.00, Sun. from 11.00. March – October weekdays until 17.00. Sun. from 14.00. November – February weekdays until 16.00. Sun. from 14.00. 2 miles west of Kingston-upon-Thames, Greater London, on A308.

Hughenden Manor. *The National Trust.* Rebuilt by Benjamin Disraeli, the Earl of Beaconsfield, and contains much of his furniture, pictures, books and other relics. Teas. Open daily, except Tue., February – December, 14.00 – 18.00 (or dusk). Sat. and Sun. from 12.30. 1½ miles north of High Wycombe, Buckinghamshire, A4128.

Knole. *The National Trust.* An enormous 15th century house with royal associations. Fine Jacobean interior and collection of furniture. Open Wed., Thu., Fri., Sat. and Bank Holiday Mon., March – December, 10.00 – 12.00 and 14.00 – 17.00. March, November and December until 17.30. Sevenoaks, Kent.

Loseley House. *J. R. More-Molyneux, Esq.* Elizabethan mansion with royal associations and panelling from Nonsuch Palace. Furniture and fine ceilings. Terrace and moat walks. Open Thu., Fri., Sat. and Bank Holiday Mon., June – September, 14.00 – 17.00. 2½ miles south-west of Guildford, Surrey, off A3100. (Guildford 62518.)

Luton Hoo. *Sir Harold Wernher, Bart., G.C.V.O.* A magnificent mansion, begun by Robert Adam, containing jewellery, paintings, tapestries and early English porcelain. Beautiful gardens. Refreshments. Open daily, except Tue. and Fri., from mid-April to September, 11.00 – 18.00. Sun. from 14.00. 2½ miles south of Luton, Beds., off A6. (Luton 22955.)

Breamore House, Hampshire

Milton Manor House. *Surgeon Capt. and Mrs. E. J. Mockler.* A 17th century house with Georgian wings. Open Sat., Sun. and Bank Holiday Mon., May – September, 14.30 – 18.00. Milton, 3 miles south of Abingdon, Berkshire, off A4. (Steventon 287.)

Penshurst Place. *Viscount De L'Isle, V.C., K.G.* Medieval and Elizabethan manor with 14th century Great Hall and

The Great Gatehouse, Hampton Court Palace

16th century formal gardens. Refreshments. Open Sat. and Sun. April to mid-September. Tue., June to mid-September, 14.00 – 18.00. August and September from 13.00. Bank Holiday from 11.30. 7 miles south of Sevenoaks, Kent, B2176. (Penshurst 307.)

Petworth House. *The National Trust.* The 17th century house built by the Duke of Somerset. State room decorations by Grinling Gibbons and a Grand Staircase painted by Laguerre. Fine collection of pictures, including Van Dyck, Turner, Gainsborough, Hals, Rembrandt and Reynolds. Open Wed., Thu., Sat. and Bank Holiday Mon., April – October, 14.00 – 18.00. 5½ miles east of Midhurst, Sussex, at junction of A272 and A283.

St. Mary's, Bramber. *Miss D. H. Ellis.* A fine example of late 15th century timber-frame building with a complete room of rare Elizabethan painted panelling, painted wall leather, costumes and handicrafts. Mature gardens. Open daily, except Mon., Easter to mid-October, 14.00 – 18.00 1 mile south-east of Steyning, Sussex, on A283. (Steyning 813158.)

Squerryes Court. *Major J. R. O. 'B. Warde, T.D.* A fine example of a William and Mary period house which has been owned by the Warde family for 200 years. Pictures, tapestries, furniture and documents of General Wolfe. Open March – October, Wed., Sat., Sun. and Bank Holiday Mon., 14.00 – 18.00. Westerham, Kent, on A25. (Westerham 2345.)

Luton Hoo
Bedfordshire

Puttenden Manor. *Brian D. Thompson, Esq.* A black and white house built in 1477 and subsequently enlarged. The interior is complete with oak beams, open fireplaces, four-poster beds, copper and wooden baths. Teas. Open Wed., Sat., Sun. and Bank Holiday Mon., Easter – mid-September, 14.00 – 18.00. Bank Holidays from 12.00. North-east of Lingfield, Surrey, off A246. (Edenbridge 2170.)

Syon House. *The Duke of Northumberland.* A fine Adam interior, elegant furniture and pictures, set in a magnificent Thames-side park. Horticultural centre. Refreshments. Open Mon. – Thu., April – September. Sun. in August and September, 13.00 – 17.00. Brentford, Greater London, off A315. (01-560 3225.)

Waddesdon Manor. *The National Trust.* Built in French Renaissance style for Baron Ferdinand de Rothschild from

63

1880–89. It includes a collection of French 17th and 18th century furniture and decorative art. British, Dutch, Flemish and Italian paintings. Extensive grounds with an aviary and a herd of Sika deer. Produce stall. Teas. Open daily, except Mon. and Tue., April – October, 14.00 – 18.00 and Bank Holiday Mon. from 11.00. 6 miles north-west of Aylesbury, Buckinghamshire, on A41. (0296-65 211.)

Mapledurham House. *J. J. Eyston, Esq.* Elizabethan mansion with fine ceilings, staircase and pictures. Beautiful private chapel and water mill beside the river Thames. Teas. Open Sat., Sun. and Bank Holidays, Easter – September, 14.30 – 17.30. Mapledurham, Oxfordshire, 4 miles north-west of Reading, off B4526. (Kidmore End 3350.)

FACTORY TOURS
AND CRAFT SHOPS

Beer. Trip lasts 2¼ hours. No children under 15. Parties only. Visits: Weekdays 14.15, Sat., 10.00, 10.30, 13.15, 14.15 and 14.30. Parties must give 9 months' notice. Maximum party number 40. Contact: Visits Section, Arthur Guinness Son & Co. Ltd., Park Royal, London N.W.10. (01-965 7700, ex 221.)

Cellos. Open any reasonable time by appointment. Alec McCurdy, Woodland Leaves, Cold Ash, near Newbury, Berkshire. (Thatchamb 3258.)

Cosmetics. No children under 10. Visits: Mon. – Thu., 14.15. Parties confined to school-leavers only. Max Factor & Co. Inc., Francis Avenue, West Howe, Bournemouth, Hampshire. (Bournemouth 25541.)

Furniture and soft furnishing weaving. Visits: Weekdays. Refreshments. Party maximum number 20. Party charge £5. Farnborough Barn Ltd., Banbury, Oxfordshire. (029-589 678.)

Garden Trugs made from willow with a chestnut rim and handle for garden and floral decor. Open weekdays 9.00 – 17.00, Sat. till 12.00. Thomas Smith Ltd., Trug Factory, Herstmonceux, Sussex. (Herstmonceux 2137.)

Harpsichords and Clavichords. Open weekdays 8.00 – 18.00, Fri. till 17.00 and Sat. till 13.00. John Feldberg, 2a Bradbourne Road, Sevenoaks, Kent. (Sevenoaks 51460.)

Meat Paste. Trip lasts 1 hour. Visits: Mon. – Fri., 10.30, 13.00, 14.00 and 15.15. Individuals only; no parties. Contact: C. Shippam Ltd., East Walls, Chichester, (Sussex 0243 85191.)

Newspapers. Trip lasts 2½ hours. No children under 16. Visits: Sun. – Wed., 20.30. Minimum age 15. Parties must give 5 months' notice. Maximum party number 12. Contact: The General Manager's Secretary, Daily Express, Fleet Street, London EC4 2NJ. (01-353 8000, ex 3629.)

Newspapers. Trip lasts 2 hours. Visits: Sun. – Fri., 20.45. Parties must give 6 months' notice. Maximum party number 10. Contact: General Manager's Secretary, The Daily Telegraph, 135 Fleet Street, London EC4. (01-353 4242, ex 127.)

Winchester

Pottery. Stoneware, especially kitchenware. Open daily 9.00 – 20.00, October – April till 18.30. St. Mary Bourne Pottery, Baptist Hill, St. Mary Bourne, Andover, Hampshire. (St. Mary Bourne 384.)

Pottery Lamp Bases, made to match interior decorator's schemes. Open weekdays 10.00 – 12.00 and 14.00 – 17.00 and other times by appointment. Tingewick Pottery, Tingewick House, Buckingham. (Finmere 250.)

Sculpture. Representational or abstract in stone, clay, wood, cold cast metals or fibreglass. Open any reasonable time by appointment. Faith Winter, Venzers Studio, Venzers Yard, The Streat, Puttenham, Guildford, Surrey. (Guildford 810300.)

Silverware. Handwrought domestic, church and ceremonial items, but no jewellery. Open any reasonable time by appointment. Geoffrey Harding, 31 The Green, Steventon, Berkshire. (Steventon 371.)

Wax Figures dressed in silks and velvets, embroidered with gold lace and pearls, using a technique of the 16th and 17th centuries. Open any reasonable

Westgate Gardens, Canterbury

time by appointment. No parties. Karin Churchill, Fern Gardens, Oxford Road, Garsington, Oxford OX9 9JT. (Garsington 378.)

Wine and wine sampling. Trip lasts 1¼ hours. Persons under 18 must be accompanied by a responsible adult. Visits: April – October, Mon. – Thu., 10.00 and 14.00 Fri. mornings only. Parties must give 1 years' notice. Party maximum number 52. Contact: The Merrydown Wine Co. Ltd., Horam Manor, Horam, Heathfield, Sussex. (Horam Road 2254.)

Woodcarving. Ecclesiastical and domestic furniture. Ivor Newton & Son, Aston Road, Haddenham, Buckinghamshire. (Haddenham 461.)

Woodcarving. Reproductions, portrait heads, modern wood sculpture and lettering. Open daily 9.00 – 18.00 by appointment only. Walter Tiffany, 34 Mill Green, Caversham, Reading.

Wrought Ironwork. Gates, balustrading, garden furniture, firescreens and work in brass and copper by Italian craftsmen. Open weekdays 8.30 – 18.30. Mario di Pinto, The New Forge, Nuneham Courtenay, Oxford. (Nuneham Courtenay 238.)

INNS AND COACHING HOUSES

Falstaff (A2, 28, 257 and 290), St. Dunstan's Street, Canterbury (Canterbury 62138). Built in 1403, it sheltered pilgrims who arrived after the city gates had been closed for the night and who might otherwise have had to sleep under the hedges. At this time it was known as the White Hart. Coach parties of up to 60 welcome, by appointment.

George Hotel (A259 and 268) High Street, Rye, Sussex (Rye 2114). A Georgian facade with a Regency assembly room complete with bow windows and music gallery and with much of the building dating from 1575. The beams are supposed to be from Elizabethan ships which defeated the Armada. Banqueting room.

Hopcrofts Holt (A423), Steeple Ashton, Oxfordshire. At one time patronised by the highwayman Claude Duval. Though modernised, it retains all the prerequisites of the traditional coaching inn. Specialities: Beef Stroganoff, steak au poivre, duckling anglaise. Dinner dances every Saturday. Car park. Coach parties up to 50 by appointment.

Ostrich (M4), Old Bath Road, Colnbrook, Buckinghamshire (Colnbrook 2628). A monastery hospice probably dating back 800 years. It fell into sad disrepute when an innkeeper murdered wealthy guests staying the night by tipping them out of bed into a vat of boiling fat. Specialist dishes: venison in port wine, jugged hare, home-made steak, kidney and mushroom pie, fillet steaks. Parking at rear of building. Coach parties of up to 36 accommodated until 23.30.

Rose and Crown (A337), Lyndhurst, Hampshire (Brockenhurst 2225). Set in the middle of the New Forest, the inn dates back to the 16th century. Coach parties welcome by appointment.

Royal Standard of England (A40), Forty Green, Beaconsfield, Buckinghamshire (Beaconsfield 382). Reputed to enjoy the distinctive name by command of Charles II who sheltered there during his flight to France in 1651. Candlelit bar with a collection of curios. The Owd Roger beer is brewed specially.

Shaven Crown (A361), High Street, Shipton under Wychwood, Oxfordshire (Shipton 330). The inn was built in the 14th century as a hostel for pilgrims to Bruern Abbey. Queen Elizabeth gave the inn to the village on condition that the profits were distributed among the poor. In 1927 the name was changed when the place was bought by a brewery, the charity receiving the sale price as capital. English cuisine, all fresh. Coach parties welcome.

The British Lion (A20), The Bayle, Folkestone, Kent. The Georgian front hides an ancient interior for the house has been an inn since 1460. Charles Dickens stayed there while writing Little Dorrit. Specialities: Home-made steak and kidney with savoury potato pie. Parking for more than one hour allowed on one side of the road only. Coach parties welcome.

The New Inn (A259), High Street, New Romney, Kent (New Romney 2332). One of the oldest inns in Kent with a Tudor entrance and, within, an attractive Georgian staircase leading to the

banqueting room. The dark oak beams and ancient cellar confirm its history as both a coaching inn and a smugglers' haunt. Parking at rear of hotel. Coach parties of up to 40 welcome by appointment.

The Royal Oak (A31, 33, 34 and 272), Royal Oak Passage, off High Street, Winchester, Hampshire (Winchester 61136). Restaurant is sited in what is reputed to be the oldest bar in England. The rest of the building dates from 1630. Luncheons only. Specialities: English home made cuisine. Coach parties of up to 28 welcome, by appointment.

The White Hart (A423), High Street, Nettlebed, Oxfordshire (Nettlebed 245). An early 16th century coaching house where the ostlers used to drink in·"the tap". The interior retains the period atmosphere. Specialities: Curries, steak and kidney pies, game in season.

The White Horse (A24 and 25), High Street, Dorking, Surrey (0306 81138). A hostelry since the 13th century, part of the existing building, including the cellars, are hewn out of the sandstone bedrock and date from the 15th century. Free house.

White Hart (A20 and 259), High Street, Hythe, Kent (Hythe 662261). A fine Elizabethan inn with the open courtyard formerly used as a market place. A door leads direct to the town hall and council chamber and one of the rooms was formerly used as robing room for aldermen. There is a superb oak staircase and 19th-century casting of the Royal Arms behind the dogs in the open hearth of the dining room, originally a kitchen. Parking in the courtyard.

White Hart Hotel (A22), High Street, Godstone, Surrey (Godstone 2521). Built in 1388, a free house since the time of Richard II. Much of the original building remains, with ancient beams and old fireplaces. Queen Victoria stayed there. Specialities: Fillet steak, escalopes of veal, entrecote au poivre. Free house.

LIGHT RAILWAYS

Hythe – Dungeness. 65 minutes each way. Service: Easter – September daily, October Sunday only. 13¾ miles of 15-inch gauge steam railway. The Romney, Hythe and Dymchurch Railway, New Romney, Kent. Telephone: New Romney 2353.

Sheffield Park – Horsted Keynes. 20 minutes each way. Service: Saturday, January – November. Sunday, February – December. Wednesday, May – October. Daily, June – September. Refreshments. Bluebell Railway Preservation Society, Sheffield Park Station, Uckfield, Sussex. Telephone: Newick 2370.

MUSEUMS

Booth Museum of British Birds. A large collection of British birds mounted in cases which represent their natural environments. Open daily 10.00 – 18.00. Winter until 17.00. Sun. 14.30 – 17.00. Dyke Road, Brighton, Sussex.

Chartwell. *The National Trust.* Sir Winston Churchill's home containing many national and personal relics. Open Wed., Thu., Sat., Sun. and Bank Holiday Mon. 11.00 – 18.00 (or dusk). Wed. and Thu. from 14.00. 2½ miles south of Westerham, Kent, off B2026.

English Rural Life Museum. *Reading University.* A national collection of material relating to the history of the English countryside, incorporating agriculture, crafts, domestic utensils and village life. Open daily, except Sun. and Mon., 10.00 – 13.00 and 14.00 – 16.30. 7 Shenfield Road, Reading.

Jane Austen's House. *The Jane Austen Memorial Trust.* Her home and garden includes a collection of portraits, documents and first editions. On view is her study and the famous creaking door which warned her of anyone approaching. Open daily, except Mon. and Tue. in November – March, 11.00 – 16.30. Chawton, 1 mile south of Alton, Hampshire, A31 and A32.

1909 40/50 hp Rolls Royce 'Silver Ghost', Montagu Motor Museum

Montagu Motor Museum & Buckler's Hard. *Lord Montagu of Beaulieu.* Over 200 veteran and vintage cars, commercial motor vehicles, motor cycles and bicycles. Models, plans and relics of ships and ship building in the 19th century, on the site of what was formerly a large shipyard. Open daily 11.00 – 13.00 and 14.00 – 18.00. 5 miles south-east of Lyndhurst, Hampshire, B3056.

Quebec House. *The National Trust.* A 16th century house where General Wolfe spent his early years. Two rooms, a hall and staircase are shown, together with some personal relics. Open Tue., Wed. and Sun., March – October, 14.00 – 18.00. Westerham, Kent.

Smallhythe Place. *The National Trust.* A half-timbered 15th century house, the home of Dame Ellen Terry from 1899 until her death in 1928. The house contains personal relics of Dame Ellen, Mrs. Siddons, Garrick and other famous stage personalities. Open daily, except Tue. and Fri., March – October, 14.00 – 18.00 (or dusk). 2½ miles south of Tenterden, Kent, on B2082.

PARKS AND GARDENS

Borde Hill Garden (Haywards Heath 50326). Gardens and woodlands set around a period house. Particularly fine displays of magnolias, camellias, rhododendrons and azaleas during April, May and June. Teas. Open Sat., Sun., Wed. and Bank Holiday Mon., April – September, 14.00 – 19.00. Until 17.00 in September. ½ mile from Haywards Heath, Sussex.

Furzey. Heathers and azaleas February – June, rhododendrons, autumn foliage. Open daily all year, 10.00 – dusk. Minstead, near Lyndhurst, 1 mile west of Cadnam, Hampshire.

Pusey House Gardens. Fine trees, watergardens surrounding a lake, extensive shrubberies. Particularly beautiful in mid summer with the herbacious borders and rose garden. Open Wed., Thu. and Bank Holidays, April – mid-October, 14.00 – 18.30. Faringdon, 12 miles west of Oxford, off A420.

Royal Botanic Gardens (01-940 1171). The world-famous Kew Gardens, with impressive avenues and lakes. 45,000 different plants and a herbarium. Refreshments. Open daily all year, 10.00 – 16.00, summer until 20.00, glasshouses until 13.00. Kew, 1 mile from Richmond, Surrey.

Savill Garden. Extensive woodland gardens. Refreshments. Open daily March – October, 10.00 – 18.00. Ap-

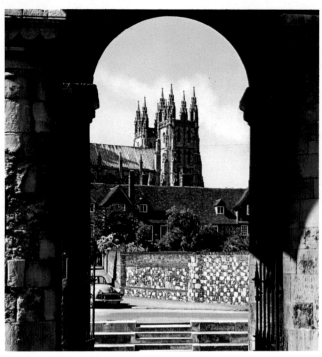

Canterbury

proach by Wick Road, Great Park, Windsor.

University Botanic Gardens. Set out so as to show history of flowers and the link between wild and cultivated flowers. Open daily 8.00 – 17.00. Sun. 10.00 – 12.00 and 14.00 – 18.00. October – April until 16.00. Oxford.

Winkworth Arboretum. Azaleas and rhododendrons in May, brilliant autumn foliage in October. Open daily all year. 3 miles south-east of Godalming, Surrey.

Wisley. Royal Horticultural Society experimental garden with trials of selected ranges of flowers and vegetables. Fine displays of rhododendrons. Refreshments. Open daily all year, 10.00 – 19.30. Sun. from 14.00. Near Ripley, Surrey.

PLEASURE FLIGHTS

Blackbushe Airport. Aeromart Flying Club, near Camberley, Surrey (Yateley 3753). Flights at weekends. Refreshments.

SPAS AND HISTORIC CITIES

Chichester. The Romans called their settlement Noviomagnus but the city takes its name from the word the Saxons gave it: Cissa's Ceaster. There are many old buildings in the city and some particularly fine Georgian houses. Churches:

Oxford Cathedral
interior

The Cathedral; All Saint's Church. Museums: Council House; Chichester City Museum. Places of interest: Bishop's Palace; The Pallants; St. Martin's Square; The Council House; The Market Cross; Priory Park; John Edes' House; City Walls; Roman palace at Fishbourne. Racing at Goodwood.

Canterbury. Canterbury's history goes back more than 2,000 years. During the 2nd World War some of the city's ancient buildings were destroyed by enemy action but Canterbury still retains much of its medieval charm. Churches: Cathedral; Church of Christ; St. Martin's. Museums: Royal Museum; West Gate Museum; Slater Art Gallery. Places of interest: Norman Keep; St. Augustine's Abbey; Greyfriars; Blackfriars; Eastbridge Hospital; Weaver's Houses; West Gate and City Walls. Gardens: Dane John; West Gate. River trips from Blackfriars Monastery, the Weaver's, King's Bridge.

Oxford. This ancient seat of learning, on the river Thames, attracts visitors from all over the world. Churches: Christ Church; St. Mary's; St. Michael's; St. Peter's-in-the-East; All Saints. Museums and libraries: Ashmolean; University Museum; Radcliffe Camera; Bodleian Library; Rotunda. Places of interest: Sheldonian Theatre; Martyrs' Memorial; Mitre Inn; Golden Cross Inn. Colleges: All Souls; Balliol; Brasenose; Corpus Christi; Exeter; Hertford; Jesus; Keeble; Lincoln; Magdalen; Mansfield; Merton; New College; Nuffield; Oriel; Pembroke; Queen's; Christ's Church; St. John's; Trinity; Exeter; Jesus; Wadham; Worcester; St. Edmond's Hall; Hertford; Keble; Rhodes House; Lady Margaret's; Somerville. Gardens: Botanic Garden; University Park; Christ Church Meadow.

Tunbridge Wells. The medicinal qualities of the wells were discovered in the early 17th century and the town soon became fashionable with Royalty who often came to take the waters. The town is still a spa and it retains much of its ancient charm. Places of interest: The Pantiles. Gardens: Calverley Grounds Hilbert; St. John's Dunorlan; The Common; Mount Sion Grove; Grosvenor Recreation Grounds. Boat hire: Dunorlan Park.

Winchester. Winchester was formerly the Wessex capital of King Alfred and the city's close links with history have left a wealth of interesting buildings for the visitor to see, the cathedral being exceptionally beautiful. Churches: St. Bartholomew's; St. John the Baptist's; St. Lawrence's; St. Swithun's; St. Matthew's. Museums: City Museum; The Westgate Museum; Royal Green Jackets and Royal Hampshire Regimental Museums. Places of interest: St. John's Hospital; The Pentice; The House of Godbegot; The Old Guildhall; The Westgate; Castle; Wolvesey Castle; St. Cross Hospital; Hospital of St. John the Baptist. Parks: Nuns' Walk and other riverside walks.

THE SEASIDE

Bournemouth. Seaside attractions: Two amusement piers, sea trips to Isle of Wight, Swanage and Poole, also motor and speed boats, mini golf, putting, tennis, cricket, football, ice rink. Seven cinemas. Children's amusements: Sand, pony rides, boating and paddling pools. Live shows: Summer show and concerts at the Pavilion; Straight plays at the Palace Court Theatre; Ice shows at Westover; Aqua show at the Pier Approach Baths; Variety concerts at the Winter Gardens and summer show at the Pier Theatre. Dancing at the Pavilion and Royal ballrooms.

Brighton. Seaside attractions: Dolphinarium and aquarium, Black Rock swimming pool, eight cinemas, two theatres, two piers, putting, tennis, golf, Booth bird museum, horse races, Saltdean lido, sun terrace, King Alfred indoor sports centre, Lagoon, West and Palace amusement piers, pleasure flights from Shoreham Airport, Brighton Road, Shoreham. Illuminations April – October. Live shows: Variety, Palace Pier. Straight plays at Theatre Royal. Dancing at the Top Rank Ballroom and many discos. Children's amusements: Peter Pan's Playground, boating and paddling pools. Items of interest: Shoreham lifeboat and lighthouse; Pleasure flights from Shoreham Airport; Royal Pavilion; The Lanes, with antique shops.

Broadstairs. Seaside attractions: Promenade, pier, launch trips from pierhead, illuminations from Whitsun to September, putting, golf, tennis. Children's amusements: Sand, donkey rides, miniature railway, trampolines, intimate cinema. Live shows: Orchestra

The Square and Town Centre, Bournemouth

The Royal
Pavilion, Brighton

shipping, two promenade piers, two cinemas, launch trips, harbour. Children's amusements: Playground, paddling pool. Items of interest: Dover Castle; Kearsney Abbey; Connaught Park; Museum; Pencester Gardens; Russell Gardens; Town Hall; Chapel of St. Edmund.

Eastbourne. Seaside attractions: Amusement pier, launch trips from west side pier, aquarium, band, model village, two indoor swimming pools, bowls, tennis, putting, mini golf, four cinemas. Live shows: Variety, Hippodrome. Summer show, Congress Theatre. Concerts, Congress Theatre. Straight plays, Devonshire Park Theatre. Dancing: Winter Gardens and several hotels. Children's amusements: Beach, kiddies' corner, donkey and pony rides, boating pool. Items of interest: Lifeboat museum at Wish Tower; Hampden and Princes

The Harbour,
Broadstairs

and audience participation at the Pavilion and Bandstand. Dancing at the Grand Ballroom. Items of interest: North Foreland lighthouse; York Gate; 11th century Parish Church; Dickens' Bleak House; Flower Show, June; Orchestral concerts.

Deal. Seaside attractions: Promenade, pier, crazy golf, putting greens, pleasure trips, bowling, two cinemas, theatre, bingo. Children's amusements: Paddling pool, roundabouts near pier. Live shows: Variety, Astor Theatre. Disco dancing. Items of interest: Walmer lifeboat; Deal and Walmer Castles; Carnival and Regatta – July.

Dover. Seaside attractions: Passing

Parks; Pevensey Castle; Beachy Head; Towner Art Gallery.

Folkestone. Seaside attractions: Open-air bathing pool, sports centre with swimming pools, squash, tennis, badminton courts, dry ski slope, golf course, roller skating rink, Rotunda amusement park, two cinemas, bowls, croquet, pier, outdoor concerts and bingo. Day trips from the harbour to Calais, Boulogne and Ostend. Children's amusements: Beach, boating pool. Live shows: Variety, Leas Cliff Hall; Summer show, Marine Pavilion; Straight plays, Leas Pavilion. Dancing: Leas Cliff Hall and the Continental Wampach and the Grand Hotels. Items of interest: Museum and art gallery; New Metropole Arts Centre; Kingsnorth Gardens; The Leas; The Warren.

Hastings and St. Leonard's Seaside attractions: Pier, cliff walks, indoor swimming, concerts, bowls, squash, tennis, boating trips, two cinemas. Children's amusements: Miniature railway, model village, boating lake. Live shows: Pier, White Rock Pavilion. Places of interest: Castle; Battle Abbey; Old Town; Fishermen's Museum; National Chess Tournament; Town Crier's Contest in August; Fairlight Glen; Caves; Alexandra Park.

Herne Bay. Seaside attractions: Promenade pier, roller skating at central bandstand, crazy golf at Hampton Pleasure Ground, putting, tennis and boating at War Memorial Park. Illuminations: June – September; Flower gardens July, badminton, golf. Children's amusements: Trampolines, pony rides, kiddicars at the Clock Tower Gardens. Live show: Dancing, King's Hall. Items of interest: Roman fort; Reculver Saxon Church; Museum.

Littlehampton. Seaside attractions: Amusement fair, cinema, theatre, miniature and garden golf, tennis, archery, croquet, bowls. Boat trips to Arundel and Amberley. Children's amusements: Donkey rides, model boating lake, miniature railway, Mewsbrook Park play area. Live shows: Theatre: Windmill Theatre. Children's show: Windmill Theatre. Places of interest: Nautical Museum.

St. Margaret's Bay, Dover

The Carpet Gardens, Eastbourne

Clock Tower and
Castle, Hastings

The River Arun,
Littlehampton

East Beach, Herne
Bay

Margate. Seaside attractions: Amusement pier, harbour jetty, Dreamland and Cliftonville Lido amusement parks, passing shipping, dolphinarium. Launch and speed boat trips from harbour and pier. Illuminations, May – October. Children's amusements: Clean sand, kiddies' corner, donkey rides, boating and paddling pool, tidal pools, miniature zoo, trampolines. Live shows: Variety: Winter Gardens, Queens Theatre and Lido Theatre. Wrestling and band concerts: The Oval. Dancing: Dreamland, St. Mildred's Ballroom, Westgate. Items of interest: Lifeboat house; Shell Grotto; Grotto Hill; Powell-Cotton Big Game Museum, Tudor Cottage, King Street; Margate Caves, Northdown Road, Cliftonville; model village; Drapers Mill.

Ramsgate. Seaside attractions: Promenade pier, two cinemas, theatre, Pleasurama amusement park, model village, bathing pool, greyhound track, golf. Boat trips from East Pier. No-passport day-trips to Continent from Ramsgate International Hoverport, Pegwell Bay. Illuminations. Children's amusements: Sand, kiddies' corner, donkey rides, boating pool, Punch & Judy. Live shows: Dancing: Nero's Discotheque, Dixieland Showbar; Granville House Ballroom. Places of interest: Royal harbour; Viking ship "Hugin".

Sunset at Margate

H. M. S. Victory,
Portsmouth

Southsea and Portsmouth. Seaside attractions: Two amusement piers, cinemas, passing shipping, model village; crazy golf, bingo, ten-pin bowling, roller skating rink, amusement park. Steamer service to Isle of Wight; other sea trips from South Parade and Clarence Piers. Hovercraft trips to Isle of Wight. Illuminations, April – mid-October. Children's amusements: Kiddies' corner, boating and paddling pools, miniature railway, model village. Live shows: Straight plays: King's Theatre. Aqua show: Hilsea Lido. Dancing: Locarno Ballroom. Places of interest: *H.M.S. Victory* at Portsmouth Dockyard; Old Portsmouth; the Garrison and Cathedral Churches; City Museum and Art Gallery; Southsea Castle and Museum of Military and Naval History, Cumberland House Natural History Museum; Charles Dickens' Birthplace Museum; Royal Marines Museum; Eastney Barracks; Portchester Castle.

Worthing. Seaside attractions: Pier, two cinemas, theatre, Aquarena and lido, indoor and outdoor swimming pools, ten-pin bowling, putting and golf courses, orchestral concerts, pleasure flights from Shoreham Airport. Children's amusements: Brooklands Pleasure Park, Peter Pan's playground, boating and paddling pools. Live shows, Concerts: Pavilion and Assembly Hall; Plays: Connaught Theatre. Dancing: Assembly Hall. Places of interest: Museum and Art Gallery; Parsonage Row Cottages.

ZOOS

Bentley Wildfowl Collection, Halland, Lewes, Sussex (Halland 260). Five hundred birds, including 100 varieties of ornamental pheasants and peacocks. Collection of bird paintings by Philip Rickman. Feeding time: 15.00. Refreshments, seating 36. Open Wed., Sat., Sun. and Bank Holiday Mon., April – September, 11.00 – 17.30. Off A26 and A22.

Birdworld, Holt Pound, near Farnham, Surrey (Bentley 2140). Tropical birds, many flying free, set in two acres of gardens. Refreshments. Open daily 10.00 – sunset. 3½ miles from Farnham on A325.

Chessington Zoo, Surrey (Epsom 27227). Over 1,000 animals and birds. Circus during Easter fortnight and summer afternoons, fun fair, model village. Visitors may feed some of the animals. Licensed restaurants, cafeterias, marquees for parties. Open daily 9.30 – 20.00 or dusk, whichever is the earlier, winter 10.00 – 16.00. On A243.

Crystal Palace Children's Zoo, Anerley Hill, London S.E.19 (01-778 4487). Pony rides. Penguins fed 15.30. Open school holidays, weekends and Bank Holidays 11.00 – 18.00. Term time weekdays 13.30 – 17.30.

Hovercraft and Clarence Pier, Southsea

Drusillas, Alfriston, near Eastbourne, Sussex (Alfriston 234). Small zoo, farm playground. Visitors may feed the animals. Tropical butterfly presentation. Miniature railway, cottage bakery. Licensed restaurant seating 250. Open mid-February to October. 11.00 – 18.00. Off A27.

Southampton Zoological Gardens, Southampton S01 2NN (Southampton 56603). A small zoo. Feeding times start with sealions at 15.00, followed by lions and tigers. Pony rides. Also mechanical rides. Visitors can feed some animals. Light refreshments. Open daily 10.00 – sunset.

Verulamium British Wildlife Zoo, Verulamium Park, St. Michael's, St. Albans (St. Albans 54756). A small zoo specialising in British wildlife. Refreshments. Open April – October 11.00 – 13.00 and 14.00 – 18.00. Off A5.

Weyhill Zoo Park, near Andover, Hampshire (Weyhill 252). Constructed on open-pen and outside enclosure system, this small zoo specialises in European animals and birds. Also bears, leopards, etc. Seals fed 16.00. Children's corner with donkey rides during summer weekends. Visitors may feed the animals. Light refreshments, seating 50. Open daily 10.30 – 19.00, winter to 16.00. Off A303.

Windsor Safari Park. A hundred-acre estate bordering Windsor Great Park with African game, dolphinarium and monkey jungle, children's zoo and a nature trail. Refreshments. Some animals may be fed. Open daily 10.00 – dusk. Off B3022.

Zoological Society of London, Regent's Park (01-722 3333). 6,000 animals in one of the largest collections in the world. 11.30 elephants' bath time. Chimpanzee intelligence tests at children's zoo at 12.00, 14.00. Chimpanzee tea party 16.00, winter at 15.00. Penguins at Penguin Pool fed at 14.30 and at Mappin Terrace at 14.45. Eagles fed at 15.30, except Wed., winter at 15.15. Lions and tigers fed, except Wed., at 14.00, winter at 15.00. Sealions, except Fri., at 12.00, winter at 14.30. Reptiles, Fri. only, at 14.30. Shetland pony and donkey rides, Sun. 11.30 – 12.00 and 13.15 – 15.45, Easter – October. Llama trap and camel rides, daily, except Sun., at 13.45 – 15.45, Easter – September. Licensed catering, seating 200. Open daily 9.00 – 19.00 or dusk, whichever is the later. November – February from 10.00.

AREA EIGHT

Wiltshire, Dorset, Somerset, Devon, Cornwall.

CASTLES

Sherborne Castle. Built by Sir Walter Raleigh in 1594 and enlarged in 1625. Home of the Earls of Bristol and the Digby family since 1617. Fine furniture, porcelain and pictures. Grounds landscaped by "Capability" Brown. Teas. Open Thu., Sat., Sun. and Bank Holiday Mon., Easter – September, 14.00 – 17.00. Sherborne, Dorset, 5 miles east of Yeovil, off A30.

CAVES

Cox's Cave, Cheddar, Somerset. (Cheddar 742345.) Trip lasts 25 mins. Party maximum 40. Open daily Easter – October, 10.00 – 18.00.
Gough's Cave, Cheddar, Somerset. (Cheddar 742343.) Trip lasts 30 mins. Party maximum 80. Refreshments, seating for 500. Open daily 10.00 – 19.00, winter until 16.30.

Transformation
scene, Cox's Cave

Throne of Fairyland.
Wookey

Insignia, Wookey

Wookey Hole Caves, Wells, Somerset. (Wells 72243.) Trip lasts 30 mins. Party maximum 30 per guide. Also swimming pool and Titania's Palace of historical miniatures. Refreshments, seating for 200. Open daily 9.00 – 19.00.

COUNTRY HOUSES

A la Ronde. *Miss S. Tudor.* A building resembling the circular San Vitale at Ravenna with rooms radiating from a central hall. Open Wed., May – September. Tue. and Thu.; June – September, 10.00 – 12.00 and 14.00 – 17.00. North of Exmouth, Devon, off A377.

Athelhampton. *Robert Cooke, Esq., M.P.* Medieval battlemented house with a 15th century Great Hall. Tudor Great Chamber, fine furnishings, formal and landscaped gardens. Teas. Open Wed. and Thu. and Bank Holiday. Easter – September, 14.00 – 18.00. Puddletown, Dorset, 5 miles north-east of Dorchester, on A35. (Puddletown 363.)

Avebury Manor. *Sir Francis Knowles.* An Elizabethan manor with fine panelling and plaster work, collection of furniture and porcelain. Topiary and tulip gardens. Open daily, except Tue., May – August. Sat., Sun. and Bank Holiday Mon., April – September, 14.00 – 18.00. Avebury, Wiltshire. 6 miles west of Marlborough, off A4. (Avebury 203.)

Buckland Abbey. *The National Trust.* Originally a 13th century monastery, converted into a house by Sir Francis Drake on return from his voyage round the world, containing his drum and other mementos. Models of ships. Refreshments. Open daily Easter – September, 11.00 – 18.00. Sun. from 14.00. 11 miles north of Plymouth, Devon, off A386.

Cadhay. *Lady William-Powlett.* Elizabethan manor with an earlier timber-roofed Great Hall. Open Wed. and Thu. mid-July to August Bank Holiday Sun. and Mon., 14.00 – 18.00. Ottery St. Mary, Devon, off A30. (Ottery St. Mary

Longleat House. *The Marquess of Bath.* A 16th century Renaissance house with a Great Hall and Italianised state rooms. The house contains a fine collection of books and pictures. The parkland, which was originally landscaped by "Capability" Brown, now includes reserves for big game. Refreshments. Open daily, 10.00 – 18.00, winter until 16.00. 4 miles south-west of Warminster, Wiltshire, off A362. Maiden Bradley 303 (House), 328 (Lion Park).

The Manor House. *Col. F. Claridge.* Largely constructed in the 16th century with fine panelling, woodwork and doors. Period furniture and silver. Open daily 11.00 – 17.00. Sandford Orcas, Dorset, 3 miles north-west of Sherborne on B3145 or B3148. (Corton Denham 206.)

Wilton House. *The Earl of Pembroke.* The present house was built by Inigo Jones to replace an earlier Tudor house which had been destroyed by fire. Outstanding collection of pictures, furniture, porcelain and other art treasures. Stately grounds with 300-year-old cedars and a Palladian bridge. Garden centre. Refreshments. Open daily, except Sat. and Mon., from April – September, 11.00 – 18.00. Sun. from 14.00. 2½ miles west of Salisbury, Wiltshire, A30. (Wilton 3115.)

FACTORY TOURS AND CRAFT SHOPS

Carpets. Trip lasts 1 hour. Visits: Mon. – Fri., 9.30 – 11.30 and 14.00 – 16.00. Parties must give 2 week's notice. Maximum party number 35. Contact: Axminster Carpets Ltd., Gamberlake, Axminster, Devon. (Axminster 2244.)

Carved Toys. Rocking horses and other wooden toys, screen prints. Open any reasonable time by appointment. Dobbin Designs, Churchtown House, Gwithian, Hayle, Cornwall. (Hayle 2536.)

Buckland Abbey

State Drawing Room, Longleat

Corn Dollies. Traditional and modern. Also book illustrations, engraved prints and hand spun, hand woven materials for shoulder bags, ties, etc. Open any reasonable time by appointment. Jacquie Baker, 54 The Avenue, Yeovil, Somerset. (Yeovil 22751).

Doll Houses and model houses with furniture and fittings to scale in styles from the 16th century. Open daily, except Tue., 8.30 — 18.00, Sun. 10.30 –

The East Front,
Wilton House

13.00. Den & Paul Young, 73 Broadway, Frome, Somerset. (Frome 2345).

Embroidery. Lampshades, complete lamps and other items for interior decor. Open any reasonable time by appointment. Mrs. Oenone Cave, Rambler Studio, Holford, near Bridgwater, Somerset. (Holford 315).

Gemstones. Polished agate paperweights, dishes, penstands, stone carvings, crystals, polished gemstones. Open weekdays 9.00 – 17.00, Thu. till 13.00. Kernowcraft Rocks & Gems Ltd., 9 Old Bridge Street, Truro, Cornwall. (Truro 2695.)

Leatherwork. Upholstery, falconry furniture, fishing tackle, suede and leather clothing and travel goods. Open weekdays 9.00 – 17.00, Wed. till 13.00. Leathercraft, 78-9 High Street, Marlborough, Wiltshire. (Marlborough 2065.)

Pottery. Hand-thrown traditional earthenware and saltware. Open any reasonable time but prior enquiry is advisable. John Collett, Townsend Farm, Littleton Drew, Chippenham, Wiltshire. (Castle Combe 782.)

Pottery. Stoneware tableware and individual items, also ceramic jewellery. Open: Mon. – Fri. 9.00 – 12.30 and 13.30 – 17.00. Honiton Pottery Ltd., Honiton, Devon. (Honiton 2106.)

Pottery. Trip lasts ½ hour. Visits: Mon. – Fri., 10.00 – 12.30 and 14.00 – 16.30. Parties must give 2 months' notice. Maximum party number 60. Contact: Poole Pottery Ltd., East Quay Road, Poole, Dorset.

Sheepskin, coats, hats and mitts, also suede leather goods. Open: Mon. – Sat. 9.00 – 13.00. Lynton Sheepskin Shoppe Ltd., 2 Lee Road, Lynton, Devon. (Lynton 2226.)

Sheepskin Products. Tanning, coat and footwear manufacture. Trip lasts 1½ hours. Visits: Mon. – Thu., 14.15. Refreshments. Parties must give 3 weeks' notice. Maximum party number 36. Contact: Clark, Son & Morland Ltd., Northover, Glastonbury. (Glastonbury 3291, ex 202.)

Shipswood Carver. Figureheads, stern carvings, yacht bow figures, and name boards. Open any reasonable time by appointment. Charles Moore, Treworthal Cottage, Treworthal, Ruan High Lanes, Truro, Cornwall. Veryan 294.)

Spinning Accessories. Spinning wheels, distaffs, bobbin holders. Open any reasonable time by appointment. Peter Teal, Mill House Studios, Parracombe, Devon. (Parracombe 357.)

Weaving. Floor rugs, wall hangings, shoulder bags and cushions. Also heraldic embroidery. Open: Easter – Christmas, any reasonable time by appointment. Berowald Innes, Pinkney Pound, near Sherston, Malmesbury, Wiltshire. (Sherston 373.)

Weaving. Natural dyed wool in tweeds for wraps, knee rugs and scarves, etc. Open any reasonable time by appointment. Quantock Weavers, The Old Forge, Plainsfield, Over Stowey, near Bridgwater, Somerset. (Spaxton 239).

Wooden Toys, with the accent on natural finished woods, boats, vehicles, Noah's Ark, hand-sculptured wooden animals, Nativity sets. Open: Mon. – Sat. 9.30 – 13.00 and 14.00 – 18.00. Woodpecker Toys, Burvill Street, Lynton, Devon. (Lynton 2375.)

INNS AND COACHING HOUSES

King's Head Hotel (A37 and 139), High Street, Wells, Somerset (Wells 72141). It is actually older than the cathedral, having been built as a refectory for the monks engaged in the building. It has a fine 14th century timbered roof. The landlord is the fifth generation to run the hotel. Specialities: Chop suey, chow mein, curries, Chinese dishes and English grills. Coach parties up to 50 welcome.

Punch Bowl (Off A387 and 390), Lanreath, near Looe, Cornwall (Lanreath 218). Licensed in 1620, landlords once mixed the coaching trade with smuggling and it has also been the local court. There is a fine wrought iron sign. Summerhouse and garden for children. Specialities: Local salmon, chicken in cider. Free house. No coach parties.

Three Tuns (A39, 361 and 377) High Street, Barnstaple, Devon (Barnstaple 3637). Built in the 15th century by a prosperous merchant, it claims to be the oldest house in the oldest street in the oldest borough in England.

White Hart (A30 and 38), South Street, Exeter (Exeter 79897). Erected in the 14th century as a resting house for monks, it is centrally situated within the old city wall. There is a 14th century wine room. From here, during the 17th and 18th century ale was passed through the window to passengers not having time to dismount from the many coaches halting there for a change of horses. Free house. Parking at rear of building.

Ye Old Llandoger Trow (A4, 38, 370, 420 and 432), 5 King Street, Bristol. For 300 years a seafarers' inn, at one time meeting place of the Bristol slave traders and also often raided by press gangs and consequently furnished with a secret staircase so that customers could escape. Reputed to have been frequented by the pirate Mary Read, also considered to be the original of the Spyglass Inn in Treasure Island. Daniel Defoe stayed there when writing Robinson Crusoe. Coach parties of up to 40 welcome.

MUSEUMS

Admiral Blake Museum. The 15th century birthplace of the admiral with displays of relics, maps and prints. Open daily 10.00 – 13.00 and 14.00 – 17.00. Tue. until 13.00. Blake Street, Bridgwater, Somerset.

Clouds Hill. *The National Trust.* The former home of T. E. Lawrence (Lawrence of Arabia), furnished as when he

Pulteney Bridge and River Avon, Bath

lived there. Open Sun., Wed. and Thu. 12.00 – 16.00 April – September. 9 miles east of Dorchester, Dorset, on B3390.

Museum of Costume. A major display of costumes covering all aspects of fashion from the 17th century to the present day. Open daily 9.30 – 18.00. Sun. from 11.00. Winter 10.00 – 17.00. Sun. from 11.00. Assembly Rooms, Alfred Street, Bath.

PARKS AND GARDENS

Bicton Gardens Arboretum (Budleigh Salterton 2820). Gardens, arboretum and light railway. Refreshments. Open daily April – mid-October, 14.00 – 18.00. May – mid-September, from 11.00. East Budleigh, Devon.

Clifton Suspension Bridge from Ashton meadows, Bristol

Compton Acres Gardens (Canford Cliffs 78036). Japanese and Italian gardens, bronze and marble statuary. Refreshments. Open daily April – October, 10.30 – 18.30. Canford Cliffs, Poole, Dorset BH13 7ES.
Tapeley Park. Italian style gardens, extensive woodland walks and magnificent views of the estuary of the Taw and Torridge. Teas. Open daily, except Mon. and Sat., June – mid-September, 14.00 – 18.00. Instow, 5 miles south-west of·Barnstaple, Devon, off A39.
Trengwainton Gardens. Shrubs and trees from all over the world, particularly New Zealand, Australia, Chile, Burma and the Himalayas. There is also a fine collection of rhododendrons. Open Wed., Thu., Fri., Sat and Bank Holiday Mon, March – September, 11.00 – 18.00. 2 miles north-west of Penzance, Cornwall, on B3312.

PLEASURE FLIGHTS

Plymouth Airport. Plymouth Aero Club (Plymouth 72752). Flights daily, except Mondays. Licensed restaurant.
Weston Airport. Achilles School of Flying Ltd., Weston-Super-Mare (Weston 28387). Flights Whitsun – September, other months by arrangement. Licensed bar and snacks.

SPAS AND HISTORIC CITIES

Bath. Bath, with its famous hot springs, was once a Roman city. It was popularized as a spa by Beau Nash in the 18th century and contains some of the finest Georgian architecture in Britain. Church: The Abbey. Museums and art galleries: Holborne of Menstrie; Museum of Costume; Victoria Art Gallery. Places of interest: Pump Room and Great Roman Bath; Pulteney Bridge; Assembly Room; Guildhall banqueting room; Lansdowne and Royal Crescents. Gardens: Parade; Royal Victoria Park; Henrietta Park; Sydney Gardens; Botanical Gardens. Boat hire at Bathwick and Newbridge. Bath Festival held annually in June.
Bristol. The historic port and city of Bristol has long been an important centre. It offers excellent shopping and sight-seeing facilities for its visitors. Churches: The Cathedral; St. Mary Redcliffe; St. Stephen's; St. Thomas' Museum: City Art Gallery. Places of interest: Westbury College; Clifton Suspension Bridge; Brunel's "Great Britain"; Blaise Castle; St. Nicholas' Almshouses; The Runner Inn; Old Market Street; St. Bartholomew's Hospital.
Exeter. The ancient city of Exeter has much to offer the visitor and is within easy touring distance of the Dartmoor National Park. Churches: The Cathedral; St. Pancras; St. Michael's; St. Martin's; St. Mary's Steps. Museums: Royal Albert Memorial Museum; Historical Museum; The Maritime Museum; Topsham Museum. Historical buildings: The Guildhall; City Walls; Parliament Street; St. Martin's Well; Mol's Coffee House; Annivellers' Refectory; Tucker's Hall; The Custom House; Underground Passages; White Hart Inn; Ship Inn; Wynard's Almshouses; Turk's Head; The Quay. Gardens: Rougemont Gardens. Castle ruins. Roman pavement.

Museum of Costume, Bath

The Cathedral Yard, Exeter

The Old Pier,
Weston-super-Mare

Church steps,
Minehead

Salisbury. A delightful city whose architecture gracefully spans the centuries. The cathedral has the highest spire in Britain. Churches: The Cathedral; St. Martin's; St. Edmund's; St. Thomas's Church. Museums: Salisbury and South Wilts.; Cathedral Library. Historical buildings: Old Sarum Fort and Castle; Mompesson House; The Guildhall; Banqueting hall of John Halle; House of John A'Port; Shoemakers' Guildhall; The Council House; Joiners' Hall. Old inns: King's Arms Inn; Old George; Red Lion; Haunch of Venison. Places of interest: Cathedral Close; St. John Street; St. Ann Street; Poultry Cross; Market Place; City Rampart. Gardens: Queen Elizabeth Gardens; Winston Churchill Gardens; Victoria Park. Boat trips: Avon Boat House.

THE SEASIDE

Clevedon. Seaside attractions: Passing shipping, dinghy sailing, Green Beach, launch trip from Pier Beach, putting, cinema. Children's amusements: Boating, paddling pool, miniature railway, Mobo toys, playpen. Items of interest: St. Andrew's Parish Church; Coleridge Cottage; Clevedon Court; Walton Castle.

Minehead. Seaside attractions: Amusements, cinema, theatre, crazy golf, putting, cricket. Launch trips from harbour and promenade. Children's amusements: Sands, kiddies' corner, donkey and pony rides, boating and paddling pool, miniature railway, model village. Live shows: Variety, Gaiety Theatre. Aqua shows: Esplanade swimming pool. Items of interest: Lifeboat house; 15th century harbour; Fisherman's Chapel; Thatched cottages, Quay Street; 15th century Quirk's Almshouses; Church steps; Dunster Castle.

Weston-Super-Mare. Seaside attractions: 2 amusement piers, model village, two cinemas, two theatres, mini-zoo and aquarium, golf and putting, tennis, riding, Marine Lake boating, motorboat trips, pleasure flights by Achilles School of Flying, Weston Airport. Illuminations, Whitsun – October. Children's amusements: Clean sands, Punch & Judy, donkey and pony carriage rides, model railway. Live shows: Variety: Knightstone Theatre. Musical entertainment: Rozel Musical Garden. Dancing: Winter Gardens. Places of interest: Birnbeck Pier lifeboat house; Iron Age encampment; 1,000-year-old church at Uphill; Grove Park; Winter Gardens; Museum and Art Gallery; Brean Down.

ZOOS

Cricket St. Thomas Wildlife Park, Chard, Somerset (Winsham 396). Wild life park, pets' corner, aquarium, reptiles and nocturnal cave, farm with glass-walled milking parlour. Sealions, zebras, deer, etc. Set in the spacious grounds of the former home of Admiral Hood. Refreshments. Open daily 10.00 – 18.00. 3 miles from Chard, on A30.

Exmouth Zoo (Exmouth 5756). A small general zoo. Open 10.00 – 17.00 or dusk.

Longleat Safari Park, Longleat, Warminster, Wiltshire (Maiden Bradley 328). Large game reserve with lions, elephants, giraffes, white rhinos, ostriches and monkeys roaming free. Safari lake trips to see hippos, chimps and sealions. Pets' corner and donkey rides. Miniature railway, amusements, and Longleat House. Licensed refreshments seating 800. Open daily 10.00 – 18.00 4 miles south-west of Warminster, off A4.

Merley Bird Gardens, Merley, near Wimborne, Dorset (Wimborne 3790). Set in 3½ acres of walled gardens. No steps or inclines. Light refreshments, seating 100. Open daily 10.00 – 19.00. On A349.

Newquay Zoological Gardens (Newquay 3342). Small zoo with a comparatively wide variety of animals. Seals fed at 15.45, winter at 14.45. Visitors can feed the animals. Refreshments, seating for 50. Open 10.00 – dusk.

Paignton Zoological & Botanical Gardens (Paignton 57479). World-wide collection of animals, set in 100 acres of exotic garden. Children's pets corner and playground. Miniature railway. Visitors may feed some of the animals. Licensed restaurant seating 400, picnic lawns. Open daily 10.00 – dusk.

Plymouth Zoological Gardens (Plymouth 51375). Collection of camels, giraffes and rare antelopes. Penguins and sealions fed 10.30 and 15.00. Some animals can be fed. Donkey rides. Light refreshments, picnic area. Open daily 10.00 – sunset.

Tropical Bird Gardens, Rode, near Bath, BA3 6QW (Beckington 326). Over 180 species of brilliant and exotic birds, many flying free, in 17 acres of grounds with ornamental lake and flower gardens. Pets' corner. Bird food available. Light refreshments. Open daily 11.00 – 19.00 or sunset, whichever is earlier. 5 miles from Frome, off A36.

Tropical Wildlife Gardens, Harbour View, Ilfracombe, Devon (Ilfracombe 2702). A small collection of animals shown in maximum freedom in picturesque gardens. Visitors may feed some of the animals. Restaurant. Open daily 10.00 – 18.30.

Woolly Monkey Sanctuary, Murrayton, near Looe, Cornwall (Looe 2532). The only protected natural colony of monkeys in the world, and visitors can walk among the inhabitants. Mother monkeys and their babies. Prairie dog colony, macaws, donkeys, Chinese geese and wild fowl. Visitors can feed the animals under supervision. Talks given daily. Light refreshments. Open daily Easter – October 10.30 – 18.00. 2 miles east of Looe on B3253.

AREA NINE

North Scotland.

CASTLES

Braemar Castle. *Capt. A. A. Farquharson of Invercauld.* Built by the Earl of Mar and burned in 1689 by the Black Colonel, John Farquharson. Repaired after the 1745 uprising and later transformed into a private residence. Centre tower and underground prison. Open daily May – September, 10.00 – 18.00. ½ mile northeast of Braemar, Aberdeenshire, on A93.

Braemar Castle and the River Dee

Craigievar Castle. *The National Trust for Scotland.* A tower house, unaltered since its completion in 1626. There are magnificent moulded plaster ceilings. Open Wed., Thur., and Sun. from May – September. Sat. July – August, 14.00 – 19.00. 5 miles north of Lumphanan, Aberdeenshire, off A980.

Druminnor Castle. *Miss J. Wright.* Built in 1440 and stronghold of the Clan Forbes. Recently restored. Open Sun. from Whitsun – October, 14.00 – 19.00.

1 mile from Rhynie, Aberdeenshire, off A97.

Eilean Donan Castle. *J. D. H. MacRae, Esq.* A 13th century stronghold built on a rocky islet between two lochs by King Alexander II to keep out the Danes. In the 18th century the castle was garrisoned by Spanish Jacobite troops. Teas. Open weekdays from Easter – September, 10.00 – 12.30 and 14.00 – 18.00. Wester Ross, Ross and Cromarty, 8 miles east of Kyle on A87.

COUNTRY HOUSES

Cullen House. *The Earl of Seafield.* In a beautiful setting, the house contains a valuable collection of portraits, furnishings, tapestries and other art treasures. Teas. Open Wed. and Sun., June – September. Thu., June – August, 14.00 – 17.00. ½ mile from Cullen, Banffshire, off A98.

FACTORY TOURS
AND CRAFT SHOPS

Carving in wood, marble and slate. Also wood engravings, postcards and Christmas cards. Open: Daily June – August, otherwise Tue – Sat., 9.00 – 17.00 Woodcarvers Shop, Bayview Road, Cullen, Banffshire AB5 2SB. (Cullen 563.)

Fish. Lobster and shellfish processing. Trip lasts 30 mins. Visits: Mon. – Fri., any time. Parties must give 3 days' notice. Maximum party number 25. Contact: Orkney Fishermen's Society Ltd., 26 Alfred Street, Stromness, Orkney. (Stromness 375.)

Marbleware. Jewellery, paper knives, table lighters and thermometers made from the local Serpentine Portsoy marble. Neighbouring pottery also open to the public. Open: Weekdays 8.30 – 17.00. The Marble Workshop, Shorehead, Portsoy, Banffshire. (Portsoy 404.)

Metalwork. Copper and bright pewter, costume jewellery, wine coasters, table mats, fruit bowls, wall plaques. Open: Daily in summer, 10.00 – 13.30, winter by appointment only. Stuart Fountain, Bridge Street, Ballater, Aberdeenshire. (Ballater 410.)

Weaving. Hand woven tweeds, dress materials and suitings in traditional and modern colours. Open: Any reasonable time by appointment. Russell Gurney Weavers. Brae Croft, Muiresk, Aberdeenshire. Turiff AB5 7HE. (Turriff 3544.)

Whisky. Trip lasts 1 hour. No children under 11. Visits: Mon. – Fri., 10.00 – 16.30. Parties must give one days' notice. Maximum party number 40. Contact: William Grant & Sons Ltd., Glenfiddich and Balvenie Distillery, Dufftown, Banffshire. (Dufftown 305.)

Wood Turning. Tableware, bowls, egg cups, stools, coffee tables, model spinning wheels. Open daily 10.00 – 20.00, May – October. Woodturner's of Brodie, Brodie by Forres, Morayshire. (Brodie 339.)

Woollens. Trip lasts 30 mins. Visits: Mon. – Fri., 8.00 – 12.30 and 13.30 – 17.00. Sat. till 12.30. Maximum party number 60. Contact: James Pringle Ltd., Holm Woollen Mills, Inverness. (Inverness 31042.)

Woollens. Trip lasts 45 mins. Visits: Mon. – Thu., 9.30, 10.30, 11.30, 14.00, 15.00, 16.00 and 16.30, Fri. till 12.00. Parties must give 2 weeks' notice. T. M. Hunter Ltd., Sutherland Wool Mills, Brora, Sutherland. (Brora 366.)

MUSEUMS

Inverness Museum. A large collection of Jacobite and Royal Stuart exhibits, paintings, arms and armaments of the Highlands, costumes, tartans, social and agricultural accoutrements. Open daily, except Sun., 9.00 – 17.00. Castle Wynd, Inverness.

HISTORIC CITY

Aberdeen. Known as the "Granite City" Aberdeen is Scotland's major seaside resort, containing much that is of interest to the visitor. St. Machar's Cathedral was founded in the 12th century. There are two other cathedrals – St. Mary's (R.C.) and St. Andrew's

Union Street, Aberdeen

(Episc.). Museums: Art Gallery and Museum, Schoolhill; Provost Skene's House, City centre; University Natural History Museum, Marischal College; Gordon Highlanders' Regimental Museum, Bridge of Don. Historical buildings: Town House; Marischal College; King's College; Mercat Cross; Robert Gordon's College; St. Nicholas Church tower; The Harbour; The Fish Market; Old Tolbooth. Gardens: Duthie Park, including the Winter Gardens; Johnston Gardens; Steward Park; Victoria and Westburn Parks; Union Terrace Gardens; Hazelhead, including the Zoo; Seaton Park; Walker Park and Cruickshank Botanic Gardens.

ZOO

Aberdeen Zoo, Hazlehead (Aberdeen 39369). Small zoo. Guided tours optional. Seals fed at 11.30 and 15.30. Refreshments. Open daily 10.00 – dusk or 20.30, whichever is earlier.

AREA TEN

Central Scotland.

CASTLES

Blair Castle. *The Duke of Atholl.* A 13th century fortress largely rebuilt in Victorian times containing collections of china, lace, tapestry, Jacobite relics, arms and armour, pictures and family possessions. Refreshments. Open Sun. and Mon., Easter to mid-October. Tue. – Sat., May to mid-October, 10.00 – 18.00. Sun. from 14.00. Blair Atholl, Perthshire, 8 miles north-west of Pitlochry on A9.

Crathes Castle. *The National Trust for Scotland.* A fine Jacobean castle with remarkable painted ceilings. Formal gardens. Open Wed., Sat. and Sun., all year. 14.00 – 18.00 or dusk. Daily, May – September, 11.00 – 13.00 and 14.00 – 18.00. Banchory, Kincardineshire. 14 miles west of Aberdeen, off A93.

Doune Castle. *The Earl of Moray.* One of the best preserved medieval castles in Scotland. Built in the 14th century as a royal palace and owned by the Earls of Moray since the 16th century. Associations with Prince Charles Edward and Mary Queen of Scots. Motor museum. Open daily 9.00 – 18.00. 9 miles north-west of Stirling on A84.

Edinburgh Castle. 11th century chapel and 14th century keep although most of the building dates from the 15th to 17th centuries. The Great Hall was the parliament meeting place. Royal apartments have associations with James VI and Mary Queen of Scots. Collection of weapons and armour. Scottish regalia displayed in the Crown Room. Refreshments. Open daily, 9.30 — 18.00. Sun. from 11.00. November – April, until 17.15. Sun. 12.30 – 16.30. Castle Hill, Edinburgh.

Glamis Castle. *The Earl of Strathmore and Kinghorne.* Re modelled in the 17th century Château style with a 15th century tower. Birth place of Princess Margaret. Refreshments. Open Wed. & Thu., May– September. Sun. July – September. 14.00 – 17.30. Glamis, Angus, 12 miles north of Dundee, A928.

Inveraray Castle. *The Duke of Argyll.* Present castle was built in the 18th century. Great hall and armoury, state rooms with tapestries, pictures and furniture. Period kitchen. Teas. Open daily except Fri., April – June., April – October 10.00 – 12.30 and 14.00 – 18.00. Sun. 14.00 – 18.00. Inveraray, Argyll. 58 miles north-west of Glasgow, off A83.

Kellie Castle. *The National Trust for Scotland.* Fine example of the domestic architecture of the lowlands of Scotland. Noted for plasterwork and painted panelling. Open daily except Mon. and Tue., April – September, 14.00 – 18.00. 3 miles north-west of Pittenweem, Fife, off A921.

Blair Castle, Blair Atholl

COUNTRY HOUSES

Falkland Palace. *The National Trust for Scotland.* A hunting palace for the Stuart kings from the mid-15th century until the death of James VI. Open daily April – October, 10.00 – 18.00. Sun. from 14.00. Falkland, 12 miles north of Kirkcaldy, Fifeshire, A912. (Falkland 397.)

Hopetoun House. *The Marquess of Linlithgow.* A fine example of Adam architecture with beautiful furniture,

pictures and historical items. Deer park and nature trail. Teas. Open daily, except Thu and Fri., May – September, 13.45 – 18.15. South Queensferry, West Lothian. 12 miles north-west of Edinburgh, off M90. (South Queensferry 370 and 497.)

Scone Palace. *The Earl of Mansfield.* Largely rebuilt in 1803 incorporating parts of the 16th century palace. Steeped in Scottish history, the house contains a fine collection of French furniture, china, 16th century needlework and bed hangings worked by Mary, Queen of Scots,

ivories and various artistic ornaments. Beautiful grounds. Open daily, mid-April – September, 10.00 – 18.00. Sun. from 14.00. 1 mile north of Perth, on A93. (Scone 51416.)

The Binns. *Mrs. Dalyell of the Binns.* The historic home of the Dalyell family containing fine 17th century plaster ceilings. Open daily, except Fri., Easter – September, 14.00 – 17.30. 4 miles east of Linlithgow, West Lothian, on A904. (5433-255.)

FACTORY TOURS AND CRAFT SHOPS

Beer. Trip lasts $\frac{1}{2}$ hour. No person under 18. Visits: Mon. – Thu., 14.30 and 16.00. Parties must give 1 months' notice. Maximum party number 25. Contact: Thomas Usher & Son Ltd., Usher/Vaux Brewery, 106 St. Leonard's Street, Edinburgh. (031-667 3311.)

Beer. Trip lasts $1\frac{1}{2}$ hours. Visits: Mon. – Fri., 10.30 and 14.30. Parties must give 5 days' notice. Maximum party number 20. Contact: Scottish & Newcastle Breweries Ltd., Abbey Brewery, 111 Holyrood Road, Edinburgh 8. (031-556 2591.)

Deerskin Goods. Handbags, purses, berets, belts. Also tilt marble goods on sale. Open: Daily 8.00 – 17.00. Perthshire Crafts Ltd., The City Hall, Dunkeld, Perthshire. (Dunkeld 404.)

Glamis Castle

Glass. Trip lasts 40 mins. Visits: Mon. – Thu., 10.30 and 14.15. Parties must give 1 months' notice. Maximum party number 25. Contact: The Edinburgh Crystal Glass Co., Norton Park, Abbeyhill, Edinburgh. (031-661 1213.)

Glass. Cutting and engraving. Trip lasts 30 mins. Visits: Mon. – Thu., 14.45. Parties must give 1 months' notice. Maximum party number 25. Contact: The Edinburgh Crystal Glass Co., Eastfield, Penicuik. (031-661 1213.)

Golf Clubs, woods, irons and putters. Open: Mon. – Fri. 7.30 – 14.16. Swilken Golf Co. Ltd., Argyle Works, St. Andrews, Fifeshire. (St. Andrews 2266.)

Jewellery. Silver and enamel and small silver boxes; designs from Scottish objets trouvés and microscopic slides of plant life. Open weekdays 8.30 – 17.30 and weekends at any reasonable time by appointment. Norman Grant, Silverwells, Emsdorf Street, Lundin Links. (Lundin Links 609.)

Leathercraft. 17th and 18th century hand-tooled targe reproductions and Scottish war shields. Celtic art and heraldic work moulded, carved, tooled, stained or painted. Open any reasonable time by appointment. Lochtayside Crafts, The Old Mill, Acharn by Aberfeldy, Perthshire. (Kenmore 258).

Newspapers. Trip lasts 1½ hours. No children under 10. Visits: Mon. – Fri., 14.30 or 13.15 and 15.00. Parties must

The Royal Palace of Falkland in Fife

give 1 weeks' notice. Maximum party number 15. Contact: The Scotsman, 20 North Bridge, Edinburgh. (031-225 2468, ex. 226.)

Scone Palace from the south east

Pottery. Domestic pottery, ceramic sculpture and murals. Open: Mon. – Fri., April – September, 9.00 – 17.00. Crail Pottery, Crail, Fifeshire. (Crail 413.)

Tapestry. Trip lasts 1 hour. Visits: Afternoons only and by appointment. Parties must give 1 days' notice. Maximum party number 20. Contact: Edinburgh Tapestry Co. Ltd., Dovecot Road, Corsthorphine EH12 7LE. (031-334 4118.)

Tweeds. Visits: Mon. – Fri., 9.00 – 17.30, Sat. till 12.00. Parties must give 2 days' notice. Maximum party number 30. Contact: A. & J. Macnab Ltd.,

Slateford, Edinburgh EH14 2ET. (031-443 2255.)

Whisky. Trip lasts 1½ hours. No children under 14. Visits: Mon. – Fri., 10.30 and 14.30. Parties by appointment, maximum party number 20. Contact: Hiram Walker & Son (Scotland) Ltd., 2 Glasgow Road, Dumbarton. (Dumbarton 5111.)

MUSEUMS

Atholl Museum. *The Duke of Atholl.* A collection of arms, armour, portraits and Jacobite relics housed in Blair Castle. Refreshments. Open daily May – October 10.00 – 18.00. Sun. from 14.00. Blair Castle, Perthshire. 8 miles northwest of Pitlochry on A9.

Barrie's Birthplace. *The National Trust for Scotland.* A display of articles, manuscripts and costumes associated with the playwright J. M. Barrie. Open daily 10.00 – 17.00. 9 Brechin Road, Kirriemuir, Angus.

GARDENS

Royal Botanic Gardens (031-552 7171). 300-year-old gardens with especially beautiful and extensive rock garden, landscaped plant houses and plant exhibition hall. Refreshments. No animals. Open daily all year, 9.00 – sunset. Sun. from 11.00. Inverleith Row, Edinburgh.

Camperdown Park, Dundee

The Younger Gardens, Argyll

Younger Botanic Garden. A woodland garden on a grand scale. Rhododendrons, April – early June. Garden conifers. Open daily April – September 10.00 – 20.00. Benmore, 7 miles north of Dunoon, Argyll.

HISTORIC CITIES

Dundee. The ancient city of Dundee is an excellent place to visit with its museums, churches and other places of interest which include: Churches: The City Churches; St. Paul's Cathedral. Museums: City Museum and Art Gallery; Shipping and Industrial Museum; Spalding Golf Museum. Historical buildings: The Mercat Cross; The Howff burial ground; Cowgate Port; Broughty Castle; Dudhope Castle; Claypotts Castle; The Mills Observatory; Remains of Fintry Castle; Camperdown House.

Edinburgh. Considered by many to be one of the most beautiful cities in Europe, Edinburgh enjoys a world-wide reputation and has innumerable historical and literary associations. Churches: St. Andrew; St. Giles. Museum: Royal Scottish Museum; National Gallery; Museum of Childhood; National Museum of Antiquities. Places of interest:

The Castle; The Scott Memorial; Princes Street; Holyrood House and Park; Royal Mile; National War Memorial; John Knox's House; Parliament House; Arthur's Seat; Calton Hill; Royal Botanic Gardens; Portobello; The Forth Bridges.

ZOOS

Calderpark Zoo, Uddingston, Glasgow (041-771 1185). Medium-sized zoo with tropical and nocturnal houses, monkey and cat houses, elephants, lions and reptiles. Feeding times: 15.00 – 16.30, winter 14.00 – 15.30. Pony rides in summer months. Light refreshments, seating 100. Open daily 9.30 – 19.00, winter to 17.00. On A74.

Scottish National Zoological Park, Edinburgh. Owned by the Royal Zoological Society of Scotland, this is a traditional zoo with exhibits from all over the world but particularly interesting for the native animals including Scottish wild cats and also free-flying herons. A children's model farm in miniature is stocked with young animals so that children are encouraged to gain confidence. Visitors may feed some of the animals. Open daily 9.30 – 19.00, winter till sunset. Sun from 12.00.

AREA ELEVEN

Southern Scotland

CASTLE

Culzean Castle. *The National Trust for Scotland.* Robert Adam house in a superb setting. Refreshments. Open daily March – October 10.00 – 18.30. June–August until 19.30. 10 miles south-west of Ayr, off A77.

COUNTRY HOUSES

Abbotsford House. *Mrs. P. Maxwell-Scott.* The former home of Sir Walter Scott, containing a number of his relics and manuscripts. Teas. Open daily, mid-March – October, 10.00 – 17.00. Sun. from 14.00. 3 miles west of Melrose, Roxburghshire, off A72.

Mellerstain. *Lord Binning.* A fine Adam mansion with magnificent interior decoration and coloured ceilings. Old master paintings and antique furniture. Teas. Open daily, except Sat., May – September, 14.00 – 17.30. Gordon, Berwickshire, 7 miles north-west of Kelso, off A6089. (Gordon 225.)

Traquair House. *P. Maxwell-Stuart, Esq.* Scotland's oldest inhabited house with parts dating back to the 10th century and unaltered for over 300 years. It has sheltered 27 Scottish and English Kings. An outstanding collection of treasures including relics of Mary Queen of Scots, embroideries, glass, porcelain, paintings, and manuscripts. Open Sun. and Bank Holiday Mon., mid-May – September. Wed. and Sat., June – September, daily except Fri. 10.00 – 12.30 and 14.00 – 17.30. Innerleithen, Peeblesshire, 6 miles from Peebles on B709. (Innerleithen 323.)

Culzean Castle

FACTORY TOURS AND CRAFT SHOPS

Knitwear. Trip lasts 1¼ hours. No children under 14. Visits: Mon. – Fri., 10.30 and 14.30. Closed last two weeks July and first week August. Parties must give 6 months' notice. Maximum party number 15. Pringle of Scotland Ltd., Rodono Mills, Hawick, Roxburghshire. (Hawick 3371.)

Pottery. Stoneware domestic and individual pieces, landscape decorated plates, piggy banks, candlesticks and "feelies". Open: Mon. – Sat. 9.00 – 18.00. Ian & Elizabeth Hird, The Kelso Pottery, The Knowles, Kelso, Roxburghshire. (Kelso 2027).

Pottery. Wide range of individual and domestic pieces. Open daily 10.30 – 17.00, Sun. from 14.00, by appointment. Leonard & Patricia Hassall, The Hand Pottery Studios, Woodbush, Dunbar, East Lothian.

Weavers. Fashion fabrics. Open weekdays 8.00 – 17.30. Lammermoor Woollens, Mitchell's Close, Haddington, East Lothian. (Haddington 2207.)

Weaving. Soft and floor rugs, scarves, stoles, shawls and table mats. Specialising in hand woven christening shawls. Open: Mon. – Fri. 10.00 – 18.00 and weekends by appointment. Agnes Hamilton & Monica Hardie, Pilmuir Farm, Newton Mearns, Renfrewshire. (041-639 1845).

Whisky. Trip lasts 1 hour. No children under 11. Visits: Mon. – Fri., 10.00 – 16.30. Parties must give a minimum notice of one day. Maximum party numbers 40. Contact: William Grant & Sons Ltd., Girvan & Ladyburn Distilleries, Girvan, Ayrshire. (Girvan 3091.)

Woollens. Trip lasts 20 mins. Visits: Mon. – Thu., 9.00 – 12.00 and 13.30 – 16.30. Parties must give 2 day's notice. Party maximum number 45. Contact: Peter Anderson Ltd., Waverley Mill, Galashiels, Selkirkshire. (Galashiels 2091.)

THE SEASIDE

Ayr. Seaside attractions: Promenade pier, Churchill Barracks, Barracks amusement park, band concerts at Low Green on Sundays, crazy golf, putting, bowls, tennis, cricket, sea angling. Live shows: Variety at the Gaiety Theatre. Straight plays, Civic Theatre. Ice skating at Pleasurama. Dancing at the Pavilion. Old time dancing, Masonic Hall, Mon., Thu. and Sat. 2 cinemas. Children's amusements: Sand, kiddies' corner, children's theatre, Punch & Judy, donkey rides, miniature train, Low Green paddling pool. Places of interest: Alloway Auld Kirk, Brig o'Doon; Burns' Cottage; Auld Brig; Auld Kirk; Loudoun Hall; St. John's Tower; Wallace Tower; Tam o'Shanter Inn. Gardens: Craigie; Brig o'Doon; Belleisle Park.

Wellington Square and County Buildings, Ayr

INDEX TO ILLUSTRATIONS